AUSTRALIA
LAND OF MANY DREAMS

Published in Australia by Gordon & Gotch Ltd.

First published in Great Britain 1984 by Colour Library Books Ltd.
© 1984 Illustrations and text: Colour Library Books Ltd.,
   Guildford, Surrey, England.
Display and text filmsetting by Acesetters Ltd.,
   Richmond, Surrey, England.
Colour separations by Llovet S.A., Barcelona, Spain.
Printed and bound in Barcelona, Spain by Rieusset and Eurobinder.
ISBN 0 86283 158 X

AUSTRALIA
LAND OF MANY DREAMS

Lyall Rowe

Produced by
TED SMART and DAVID GIBBON

Published by Colour Library Books for
GORDON & GOTCH LTD

Australia has been called many things – a harsh land, the lucky country, the land of the free, a land of great distances, the land of *Waltzing Matilda* – but really it is a land of immigrants and their descendants who have made it one of the wealthy countries of the world.

Geologically Australia is probably the oldest land on earth and for millions of years it slept. Then for further millions of years it was inhabited only by animals ruled by dinosaurs.

Its first human inhabitants were the Aborigines who, thousands of years ago, island-hopped from Asia. White man from Europe followed centuries later when the British settled in Sydney in New South Wales in 1788. Since then there has been a steady flow of immigrants from many lands and today with their descendants they have given the nation a cosmopolitan population of over 15,000,000 people.

The name Australia derives from the Latin word *Australis* (southern) and was accepted by the early pioneers rather than the British Government. The latter appeared quite content with the name New South Wales, which the explorer and navigator Captain James Cook had given the Great South Land when he sailed the eastern coast of Australia in 1770.

For many years New South Wales was Australia. The colony stretched from Cape York – in the far north of present-day Queensland – to the far southern island of Van Diemen's Land – known today as Tasmania – westward to take in the Port Phillip District – which is now known as Victoria – and parts of the Northern Territory.

As the 19th century progressed and Australia became the country's accepted name, the size of the colony of New South Wales began to shrink as Tasmania, Victoria and Queensland were carved from it and separate colonies were formed. The Northern Territory was first controlled by South Australia but was later handed over to the Commonwealth Government's control. At about the same time the Australian Capital Territory was created.

Australia has a total of 7,682,300 square kilometres, of which 7,614,500 square kilometres form the mainland states and territories and the island of Tasmania comprises 67,800 square kilometres. The external territories are: Norfolk Island, Cocos (Keeling) Islands, Christmas Island, Coral Sea Island, Hear and MacDonnell Islands and the Australian Antarctic Territory. In size, Australia ranks sixth in the world. It is smaller than Brazil but larger than India; almost as big as the United States of America (excluding Alaska); about 50 per cent larger than Europe (excluding the USSR) and 32 times the size of the United Kingdom.

Nature was in a capricious mood millions of years ago when it created Australia and made it a continent as well as the world's largest island. It isolated Australia on the globe in the Southern Hemisphere and made it so big that its climatic conditions range from tropical in the north – it is only a few degrees south of the equator – to Alpine in the south, where chilly blasts from the Antarctic often remind citizens that the country has experienced Ice Ages.

Nearly two-fifths of the landmass lies within the tropics, including most of Western Australia, more than half of Queensland and almost all of the Northern Territory. The other states – New South Wales, South Australia, Victoria, Tasmania and part of Western Australia – come within the temperate zone and they enjoy mostly hot summers and cold winters.

Overall, Australia is not subject to extremes of weather. Two-thirds of the land is arid or semi-arid and, because of this, Australia is a country of urban dwellers, with about four-fifths of the population living in cities and towns. This often surprises overseas visitors who frequently imagine Australians to be mostly farmers living in a sun-burnt country.

The country is largely flat. Its highest peak is Mt Kosciusko at 2,230, metres and the Great Dividing Range, which extends from northern Queensland down through New South Wales into Victoria, is the most elevated area. The lowest point is Lake Eyre in South Australia which is 15 metres below sea level.

The country has three major land form features: the western plateau; the interior lowlands and the eastern uplands.

The western plateau includes Western Australia, the north of South Australia, the Northern Territory and small areas of New South Wales and Queensland. Its average elevation is 200 to 500 metres above sea level and much of the land is arid. Its population is small, although it is increasing due to mineral exploration.

The interior lowlands, averaging less than 150 metres above sea level, extend from the Gulf of Carpentaria to the Great Australian Bight. Used chiefly for agriculture and grazing, some areas have been made more productive by irrigation. In the centre of the continent the land is arid with a low rainfall and a very high rate of evaporation.

The eastern highlands, also known as the Great Dividing Range, extend about 2,250 kilometres from north Queensland, parallel to the eastern and southeastern coast, to central-western Victoria. The range forms a watershed for rivers that flow east to the sea or west towards the interior. A fertile coastal plain separates the mountains from the sea.

Two great ocean currents have played a major part in the country's development. One, off the east coast, originates in the tropics and flows south, increasing the water vapour in the atmosphere and thus stimulating rainfall. It has created a 'green belt' in eastern Australia. Off the west coast a cold current from Antarctica flows northwards, reducing precipitation and creating deserts.

The annual wet season in tropical Australia provides a guaranteed rainfall, but rapid evaporation makes agriculture difficult in these areas. In southern Australia the winter months generally bring rain, although rainfall is usually well distributed throughout the year, making conditions favourable for agriculture.

Australia is a country of contrasts. Extended dry spells are fairly common and these occasionally develop into severe droughts. The country is also sometimes ravaged by bushfires and swamped by floods. Occasionally, the northern sector is battered by cyclones which develop over the seas to the northeast and northwest of Australia between November and April. The frequency of cyclones and the tracks they follow vary greatly from season to season. Unfortunately, very little of this rainfall finds its way into the rivers. To combat the problem, many dams have been built, but these have only been able to retain about seven per cent of the nation's rainfall and millions of litres of water pour out to sea each year. The reserves of underground water which has percolated through the earth's surface and become stored in natural subterranean basins are of incalculable value. The inland city of Alice Springs, which gained world fame in the film *A Town Called Alice*, is fully supplied by this source of water which is suitable for human consumption. In other areas, brackish supplies are used to provide water for sheep and cattle.

In contrast to the flat and mostly featureless interior, Australia has exciting coastlines. There are rocky headlands and snow-white beaches; mangrove-lined estuaries; sand dunes and towering cliffs, alternating with green heathlands, and offshore there are islands of all shapes and sizes, together with countless coral reefs. Australia is washed by three oceans – the Pacific, Indian and Southern – and by four seas –

the Tasman, Coral, Arafura and Timor.

Compared with other continents Australia has a relatively narrow continental shelf. It is a gently sloping seabed which borders the continent to a depth of 180 metres. The shelf is only 13 kilometres wide off Cape Dromedary in New South Wales and less than four kilometres wide off Norwegian Bay in Western Australia. It broadens off Queensland, where its edge is marked by the Great Barrier Reef, and at its widest point, northwest of Bathurst Island, near Darwin, extends 400 kilometres offshore. The perimeter of the shelf from Perth to Esperance Bay and off South Australia has been found to contain spectacular submarine canyons.

The major river in Australia is the Murray, which forms the border between New South Wales and Victoria, and, with its great tributary, the Darling, which runs from the Queensland border, drains part of Queensland, the major part of New South Wales and a large part of Victoria. The Murray finally flows into an arm of the sea known as Lake Alexandrina on the eastern side of the South Australian coast. The river runs for about 2,520 kilometres, about 650 kilometres of that length being in South Australia. The Darling, upstream of its point of entry into the Murray near the New South Wales pioneering town of Wentworth, runs in two sections: the first to Culgoa – a distance of 1,390 kilometres – and then the Upper Darling, which incorporates the Barwon River and which runs for 1,140 kilometres.

In north Western Australia, rivers called the Murchison, Gascoyne, Ashburton, Fortescue, Grey, Fitzroy, Drysdale and Ord are of considerable size, as are those in the Northern Territory – the Victoria and Daly – and those on the Queensland side of the Gulf of Carpentaria, including the Gregory, Leichhardt, Cloncurry, Gilbert and Mitchell. There are many other coastal rivers and inland tributaries, particularly in New South Wales and Victoria. The rivers in the island state of Tasmania are short and rapid.

Australia has three types of lakes: true permanent lakes; lakes which, being very shallow, become mere morasses in dry seasons and even dry up completely, becoming a cracked surface of salt and dry mud, and lakes which are really inlets of the ocean opening into a lake-like expanse.

Only one-third of Australia receives an average rainfall or more than 500 millimetres a year and this is mainly in coastal areas. However, there are some wet spots. Tully, in north Queensland, has an average of 4,400 millimetres and the mountainous regions of western Tasmania have an annual rainfall of 3,600 millimetres at Lake Margaret. The Snowy Mountains area in New South Wales has registered 3,200 millimetres annually, and the mountainous areas of northeast Victoria and parts of the eastern coastal slopes often register 2,500 millimetres a year.

Australia was little affected by the gigantic earth movements which millions of years ago built the high mountain chains of other continents, and many of its mountains and hills have been worn down by wind and rain. Due to the absence of extensive mountain masses and because of the expanse of ocean to the south, Australia does not experience the low temperatures recorded on other continents.

Heat discomfort is often felt in most areas of the country. During the summer, prolonged high temperatures and humidity along the northern coasts and high temperatures over the inland areas cause physical discomfort. In winter, low temperatures and strong, cold winds over the interior in southern areas can be severe for short periods.

From the beginning of recorded time natural disasters such as floods, often caused by heavy rain blown in by cyclones from the north, droughts and bushfires, have ravaged the countryside. Bushfires have always caused much damage and misery. In an average Australian summer about 400,000 hectares of forest and grassland are burnt; often homes are destroyed and lives lost, too. Lightning and spontaneous combustion are contributing causes, but so is human carelessness. 'Burning off' land, which gets out of control, flicking cigarettes and matches from motor cars, camping fires and failure to take proper precautions on farms using machinery and equipment have all led to disaster.

Except for Tasmania and a narrow fringe bordering the southern, eastern and northern coasts, the greater part of the Australian continent receives more than 3,000 hours of sunshine each year. In central Australia and the mid-western coast of Western Australia, totals in excess of 3,500 hours occur. The west coast and highlands of Tasmania do not fare so well; they only average 1,750 hours of sunshine each year.

After its people, the soil – despite the fact that much of it is arid – is Australia's greatest resource. The hard work of the pioneers and their descendants on the land helped turn this natural asset into wealth. In the early days of white settlement the soil first played its part in wool production, but grain crops did not fare too well until settlement spread west from Sydney. In the 1850s the earth yielded gold, which boosted the country's development and now provides many other minerals including coal, iron, lead, zinc, nickel, copper, bauxite, rutile, uranium and oil. The growth and spread of the nation's population was accompanied by an increase in agricultural production with grain, fruit, sugar and dairy products as well as livestock of prime importance.

Today, Australia is recognised as one of the world's most prosperous countries; it certainly has one of the most developed economies in the world. For this Australia owes much to the British pioneers – the convicts, their guards and the free settlers – who refused to be defeated by the harsh elements they encountered in their early years in the new land. They paved the way for accomplishments which, in less than 200 years, matched the achievements of Western Europe over centuries.

In its early days rural products provided Australia's wealth, but after the gold discoveries in the 1850s the soil began to provide many other minerals which, today, are major export earners. Industry and manufacturing have also boomed in the 20th century.

Australia is built on a basement of rock called the Precambrian Shield, formed early in the earth's geological history, some 3,000 million years ago. Parts of the shield can still be seen in Western and South Australia and in the Northern Territory. During the formation of the shield no touch of green relieved the barren waste of mountains, deserts, volcanoes and steaming lava fields. Almost two million years ago, when the surrounding seas were warm, primitive forms of life such as seaweed and jellyfish first appeared. Massive volcanic eruptions poured lava over the continent. The hot layers of the primitive crust buckled and solidified, folding the lodes of gold, lead, zinc, iron and uranium. Then the mountains, born amidst volcanic fire, were slowly worn down by the elements as the upheavals of the earth became less catastrophic and early forms of animal life made their appearance on land.

Australia began to assume its more modern outline about 10 million years ago when a bridge of land connecting it with New Guinea disappeared beneath the sea. Later earth action changed the course of rivers to form a lake, covering 64,000 square kilometres in central Australia with up to 60 metres of water. Around its shores, amid flourishing eucalyptus trees, roamed giant mammals and reptiles.

Australia's isolation as a landmass for 50 million years has given it a different flora from the rest of the world. Evidence from fossils shows that plant life once conformed to the basic groups of other countries, indicating that in those times Australia had land connections with Asia. When these land links disappeared, the country and its plant and animal life were isolated. In the relatively arid conditions, the struggle for survival led to a wide range of plant life. These plants form the main part of Australia's flora; the gums and wattles predominate. Overall, Australia is rich in native plants that have developed during isolation from other continents, as well as possessing a limited representation of worldwide genera.

There are three distinct elements to the country's flora. One is the characteristic Australian flora which has adapted to heat and drought or to soils deficient in nutriment. A typical adaptation to drought is the development of foliage which withstands evaporation, making the plants well suited to survive on little water. The leaves are often small, leathery, narrow or needle-like or succulent, woolly and hairy. Australian examples include the leaves of some heaths, acacias and grevilleas.

The second distinct element is the flora of the rainforests of Queensland and northern New South Wales, which has affinities with New Guinea. These plants are Indo-Malayan in origin and reached Australia from the landmasses to the north. Typical examples include the Cooktown orchid, the Illawarra flame tree and a wide range of ferns. Finally there is the subantarctic flora, that of the beech forests and Alpine moorland, such as gentians and snow daisies.

The dominant Australian trees are eucalypts of the genus *Eucalyptus* of which there are some 500 species and varieties. They grow almost everywhere on the continent, from the wet coastal forests to the arid interior and above the snow line. They dominate 90 per cent of all the continent's forest land and are the world's tallest hardwoods.

Eucalypts thrive in tropical areas, where most rainfall is in summer, and in cooler areas with winter rainfall. The more majestic species are the mountain ash of Victoria and Tasmania – the tallest hardwood in the world – the West Australian jarrah and karri, the blue gum and Alpine ash of southeastern Australia, and the blackbutt and tallow wood of the moist forests of New South Wales and Queensland. Mountain ash trees grow to more than 90 metres and karris in Western Australia's forests average 76 metres. Eucalypts have come to be regarded as symbolic of Australia.

The isolation from other continents that influenced the development of unique forms of flora, has similarly affected Australia's fauna, which includes such remarkable animals as the platypus and echidna. They are still much like the reptiles they evolved from about 140 million years ago. Called monotremes, they are the world's only egg-laying mammals.

Australia's marsupials are also survivors from remote antiquity. A marsupial is a mammal which gives birth to its young in a very immature state, then carries and suckles it in a pouch. Australia is the world's chief habitat of marsupials and has many species, the largest family comprising at least 45 species of kangaraoo, including tree kangaroos and wallabies. The red kangaroo, which grows to two metres in height, is the largest marsupial. Other marsupials include the native cats, bandicoots and wombats. The bandicoots are nocturnal, ground dwelling and eat small animals. They usually scratch the ground for worms and beetle larvae, a habit which makes them unpopular with suburban gardeners.

One of Australia's best known marsupials is the koala, which spends almost all of its life in trees. The only time it comes to earth is to cross to another tree in its search for food. In the 1920s the koala faced extinction due to hunters seeking its fur, but stringent laws were introduced to protect them and, today, they are successfully bred on reserves on Phillip Island in Victoria and Kangaroo Island in South Australia. There is always a demand for them from zoos around the world.

The largest, wild, flesh-eating Australian placental mammal is the dingo, the wild dog, probably brought to the country from Asia by the Aborigines about 25,000 years ago.

The wild camels and donkeys of the inland are descendants of animals imported into Australia in the early days of settlement. The camel, in particular, proved ideal in the dry trackless regions of the inland and much merchandise was handled with the aid of these beasts. A camel can carry a weight of around 300 kilogrammes which, in those days, meant two bales of wool.

Other imported animals have not been as beneficial. Although the first five rabbits brought from England by the First Fleet in 1788 did not survive, in 1859 a few rabbits introduced near Geelong in Victoria rapidly multiplied into millions. Many people suppose that the virus myxomatosis eliminated the rabbit problem in Australia, but this is not so. Myxomatosis breaks out every year but it is not reducing the overall number of rabbits.

There are hundreds of species of Australian birds, including 60 species of parrot, 70 species of honey-eater, 12 species of owl, 10 of quail, 24 of hawk and eagle, 20 of duck and geese and 26 of pigeon and dove. There are two large, flightless birds: the cassowary of the tropical north, and the emu. The latter is the tallest living bird, next to the ostrich. There are three remarkable Australian mound builders: the mallee fowl, brush turkey and jungle fowl, which incubate their eggs in heaps of decaying vegetable matter. The two species of lyrebird are famous for their songs and dancing. The males in particular are talented mimics and in a 20 minute recital can make many different bird calls. Also notable are the seven species of bower bird. The males build arbors made of sticks on the ground and decorate each with feathers, flowers and small objects gathered from around human dwellings according to taste. Satin bower birds of the east coast prefer to collect objects coloured blue or light yellow.

There are more than 400 species of Australian reptile, ranging in size from tiny lizards to the fearsome, 7.5 metres long, salt water crocodile. More than half of the 120 or so species of land snake are poisonous, but only about 16 are venomous enough to kill an adult human being. The taipan found in northern Australia is one of the world's deadliest snakes and grows to about 3 metres. Other dangerous snakes include the tiger snake, king brown, death adder, black and brown snakes and the Australian copperhead.

Australia is blessed with the Great Barrier Reef, a multicoloured labyrinth stretching 2,000 kilometres along the Queensland coast. It is the largest coral reef in the world, covering about 130,000 square kilometres. It protects a large part of the Queensland coast from the direct onslaught of the Pacific Ocean's pounding surf. There are few clear, deep-water passages through the coral barrier to the open sea and only 10 well-defined breaks or openings. Trade winds sweep over the reef, which also has to face the threat of the annual summer cyclones.

Nothing that grows above the water on the Great Barrier Reef equals the beauty of the garden-like coral beds below. Dominant among the hundreds of kinds of stony coral are the brain coral, with convolutions resembling those of the human brain, and the slender, branching types of staghorn. A staghorn colony may be a uniform lavender, purple, pink, green, brown, blue or yellow or coloured in combinations such as bright green and lilac, pale yellow and rose pink. Coral polyps – living creatures mostly no larger than the head of a pin – have, in countless millions and over aeons of time, laid the foundation of the Great Barrier Reef of Australia and similar reefs of the world with their skeletons. Sea anemones, known as the 'flowers of the reef', resemble chrysanthemums and cactus dahlias and grow up to 60 centimetres in diameter. They are, in fact, animals closely related in structure to the coral polyp and are to be found swaying their colourful tentacles to the rhythm of the currents in search of prey.

When Europeans first settled in Australia the Aborigine population is believed to have numbered about 300,000. There was a drastic decline over the next 145 years, and white man's diseases and maltreatment played a major part in this. By 1933 the total was estimated to be down to 67,000. It has since risen to over 150,000.

Captain Cook reported that the Aborigines 'may appear to some of us to be the most wretched people upon the earth but in reality they are far happier than we Europeans: being wholly unacquainted with the superfluous but necessary conveniences so much sought after in Europe. They are happy in not knowing the use of them. They live in a tranquillity which is not disturbed by the inner quality of condition...'

Time has shown that the Aborigines may have been content to live the nomadic life of hunter gatherers, but they possessed a cultural tradition that had evolved over thousands of years. The migration of the Aborigines, in their various tribes, is believed to have proceeded slowly over many generations and there are three main theories about their origin. The first suggests they descended from Java Man. The second theory, which has been challenged by recent discoveries, suggests that the Aborigines are racial hybrids resulting from the migration of three separate groups: the Tasmanoids, the Murrayians and the Carpentarians. The third and more favoured theory is that the Aborigines are racially homogenous throughout the continent.

Historians are not certain when the first immigrants – the Aborigines – did their island hopping from Asia. The estimate is 40 to 50,000 years ago although there is some evidence that they arrived thousands of years earlier. There seems little doubt that the Aborigines were one of the world's first seafaring people, even though their island-hopping was only over short distances of sea, for Australia was once connected to many of the islands to its north.

For thousands of years the Aborigines were content to be hunters and collectors of food; the men did the hunting and the women were the food gatherers. The Aborigine tribes were bound together by many customs and beliefs and, isolated from the rest of the world, knew nothing of the progress of civilisation in the Northern Hemisphere. As a result Australia's development was left to the white man.

The white man may have performed economic miracles but will always have to live with the memory of the atrocities the pioneers perpetrated on the Aborigines. White men accepted the friendship that was usually offered by the Aborigines – although there were occasional violent reactions by the black man – and then mistreated them. They stole their traditional lands, murdered many of them, raped their women and spread white man's diseases among them. In Tasmania the Aborigine population ceased to exist within 70 years of the arrival of the white man.

Today, Aborigines are still seeking recognition for what they claim is their land and sacred right. They are also demanding equality in health, education and employment benefits given to the white population.

The Aborigines' main weapons for hunting and fighting were the spear and the woomera or spear-thrower. The woomera is really an extension of the throwing arm, a piece of wood about a metre long with a hooked or notched end into which the butt of a spear is fitted. By using the woomera as an aid, Aboriginals can throw a spear up to 20 metres with remarkable accuracy.

They also use two types of boomerang: the returnable and the non-returnable. The returnable boomerang is more spectacular in flight but the non-returnable is the hunting weapon. The non-returnables are between half a metre and a metre long. Their curve is much shallower than the returnable boomerang. The returnable boomerang was used mainly to drive flocks of birds into a net but the non-returnable is the more dangerous and can maim or kill an animal such as a kangaroo.

The early Aborigines believed that Yhi, the sun goddess, overcame the darkness that once shrouded Australia by flooding the earth with light, life and colour. This is part of Aborigine mythology – Dreamtime – a period when life and all that goes with it was created by the great ancestral heroes. These creations included the oceans, springs and billabongs; the mountains and outcrops of rock; the sky, sun, moon and stars and the laws that governed their existence.

An integral part of Aborigine mythology is the Totem site. Frequently, totems took the place of animals and a Dreaming was associated with a particular animal which was the Dreamtime ancestor of that particular group. Dreaming places are sacred to the Aborigines and some can only be visited by initiated males.

Many forms of traditional artistic expression in Aboriginal life have been related to the religious myths and beliefs of the Dreamtime. These include ceremonies, rituals and sacred sites containing paintings and carvings, some of which are thousands of years old. There have been many fine Aboriginal artists in modern times, perhaps the best known being Albert Namatjira, of the Aranda tribe, in Central Australia. He became famous for his watercolour landscapes.

When Governor Phillip arrived with the First Fleet, he had instructions to establish friendly relations with the Aborigines. He certainly tried, but was not very successful. He could not control the actions of the settlers and the convicts, and some of the settlers drove the Aborigines from their hunting grounds, debased them with rum, slaughtered them and raped their women.

The 20th century has shown how wrong the early settlers were in their assessment of the Aborigines. They are now recognised as a basically gentle and kind people, ingenious, adaptable and completely in harmony with their environment.

A scientist named D.J. Mulvaney, who studied them closely, wrote: 'Their responses and adjustments to the challenge of their harsh environment, and their economical utilisation of its niggardly resources, are stimulating testimony to the achievements of the human spirit in the face of adversity'.

Since the first arrival of the white man, Australia has become home to thousands of refugees from many countries. Soon after the British established a convict settlement, a flow of free settlers, many of them oppressed people from Europe, began. They overcame many privations to create a better life for their descendants. They were followed in the 19th century by people from many lands who brought with them their crafts and their culture.

Some of the first arrivals were Lutherans fleeing religious persecution in Prussian Silesia. Five hundred Lutherans from Klemzig became dairy farmers and market gardeners alongside the Torrens River in South Australia. More than 4,000 more Lutheran refugees arrived during the 1840s and, by 1850, the Hahndorf settlement had been created in the Barossa Valley, which today is famous for its wines.

Since World War Two there has been a flood of refugees, including thousands of displaced persons from Europe and, in more recent times, Vietnamese fleeing from the Communist regime which had seized power in their homeland. They mostly arrived as 'boat people'. They braved the perils of the sea in boats often unseaworthy and ran the gauntlet of pirates in the South China Sea to voyage down past Malaysia, Singapore and Indonesia to 'freedom' in Darwin, Australia's gateway in the north.

Middle East conflicts also caused 20,000 migrants to select Australia as their new home. These citizens swelled the number of immigrants Australia had sought in its post World War Two drive to boost the nation's population.

There was almost unanimous agreement in Australia in 1945 that the country had had 'a lucky escape' from invasion during the war and that its population would have to show a big increase – for to its north was almost half of the world's population living in crowded Asian countries. Only an extreme optimist would have believed that these crowded countries would allow seven million Australians to hold a sparsely populated country indefinitely.

In 1947, the Federal Labor Minister for Information and Immigration, Mr Arthur Calwell, told Australians: 'We have not unlimited time to build our strength or to plan our future. Our decisions must be the right ones or else our Australian nation might not survive beyond the lives of our children of this generation'.

In the following years, assisted migration schemes were agreed with many European countries, but for years almost half the arrivals were of British origin. The gradual easing of racial restrictions saw 40,000 non-Europeans come to Australia between 1956 and 1971.

In 1971, a census showed that the percentage of the population born in Australia had fallen from 90.8 per cent in 1947, to 80.5 per cent. A 1978 study showed that Australia had 77 per cent of people with British origins, 45 per cent coming from England. The other major ethnic groups were Italians, Germans, Dutch and Greeks. In the mining town of Mt Isa, in Queensland, citizens from more than 60 nations are today living together as a single community.

The total population of Australia reached one million in 1858, five million by 1918 and has now passed the 15 million mark. Federal Government projections say that Australia's population should reach 17 million by 1991, 18.9 million by 2000 and 22 million by the year 2021.

Waltzing Matilda is a ballad which is more popular in Australia than the National Anthem, *Advance Australia Fair*. Even the National Anthem is not accepted by many of the older residents still loyal to their British backgrounds. They prefer, and still sing, *God Save the Queen*.

Waltzing Matilda means 'humping the bluey'; an Australian slang phrase for a swag. The ballad tells the story of a swagman – and there were many of them in the latter part of the 19th century and during the major depression experienced in the 1920s and 1930s. They tramped the countryside looking for work. The swag usually contained a bundle of blankets and the owner's other worldly possessions. The 'swaggie' usually travelled alone, or perhaps with a dog as his only companion. It was rare to see a woman swaggie but occasionally during the depression days they were sighted pushing a cart or a wheelbarrow containing their belongings.

Famous Australian poet Banjo Patterson wrote the story of *Waltzing Matilda* last century after he heard the phrase during a visit to the Queensland country centre of Winton. Set to music, the words describe how a 'Jolly Swagman' camped beside a billabong – a cut off loop of a river caused by flooding – and grabbed a jumbuck (a sheep) which had come to the billabong for a drink on the land of a squatter (illegal landowner). The swagman, the song says, 'Sang as he stuffed that jumbuck in his tucker bag "you'll come a waltzing Matilda with me".' But the swagman was confronted by the squatter and the troopers. He jumped into the billabong 'and his ghost may be heard as you pass by that billabong "you'll come a waltzing Matilda with me".'

Hundreds of songs have been written by other composers hopeful that they would become distinctive Australian tunes. Records show that in 1820 a bandmaster of the 3rd New South Wales Regiment composed *The Trumpets Sound Australia's Fame*. Many others still remain popular, including *The Song of Australia* composed in 1860 by Carl Linger with words by Caroline Carleton.

For many years there have been moves to replace *God Save the Queen/King* as Australia's National Anthem and an official anthem contest was staged in the 1970s. As there was no winner, the Labor Government in 1974 conducted a public opinion poll to find out whether *Advance Australia Fair*, *Waltzing Matilda* or *Song of Australia* was preferred by Australians. Fifty-one per cent favoured *Advance Australia Fair*, and the Prime Minister, Mr Gough Whitlam, announced that it would replace *God Save the Queen*, except on royal or vice-regal occasions when both tunes would be played. A change of government followed soon afterwards and the Liberal/Country Party coalition decided that only *God Save the Queen* would be played on royal and vice-regal occasions. Public debate continued, so the government in 1977 held an anthem poll referendum including *God Save the Queen* in the list of the songs used in the 1974 poll. The winner was *Advance Australia Fair* which received about 43 per cent of the vote. *God Save the Queen* received about 18 per cent.

Australia is a wealthy country, even though the nation often feels the effects of the economic downturns that strike fairly regularly in other parts of the world and often occur when Australia is in the grip of another drought. Thanks for the wealth must go to the white pioneers and their immediate descendants, as they did the groundwork necessary to build the nation.

Despite its lonely and lowly past, Australia has developed into one of the great trading nations in the world, with a voice gathering momentum in world affairs.

For years Australians literally 'lived off the sheep's back', but in recent times wool prices have been in decline and woolgrowers have claimed that farmers can earn more money from growing wheat and other crops. In the 1950s the value of wool produced in Australia was more than four times that of wheat. Today, wheat often produces twice wool's export earnings.

Australia has also become one of the world's most industrialised nations, with almost 30 per cent of the work force engaged in secondary industry.

Australia's earliest industries were glassmaking, tanning, weaving, flour milling, sugar refining and pottery. In 1915, the Broken Hill Proprietary Company opened Australia's first steel works at Newcastle in New South Wales. By 1968 cars, chemicals, electric and electronic products, and iron and steel made up 32 per cent of Australia's manufacturing output and, in the same year, figures showed that the share of total output from the less sophisticated food, drink, tobacco, textiles and clothing industries had fallen from 32 to 23 per cent.

Although gold made the major impact in mineral discoveries in the 19th century, silver and lead helped create giant complexes at Broken Hill in New South Wales and Mt Isa in Queensland; copper caused the west coast of Tasmania to be peopled; iron ore opened up the northwest of Western Australia and bauxite led to the creation of Weipa, in Queensland's Gulf of Carpentaria. Australia was once the world's major supplier of tin, and, in the stormy waters of Bass Strait off the Victorian coastline, a major discovery of oil is helping to keep down Australia's import bill.

Through much of the 19th century the colonies were divided by many kilometres of wilderness, and travel between the towns, when it was possible, was mainly by ship. Bullock wagons were used to transport goods hundreds of kilometres, although towards the end of the 19th century steamer traffic on the major rivers helped move the wool and other products resulting from the spread of settlement. Many outback towns owe their existence to wagons drawn by bullocks roped in pairs with the driver known as a 'bullocky'; usually a ribald character famous for his lewd language. His dress was often a red shirt, plaited cabbage tree hat and moleskin trousers. His whip measured about five metres. The roads built before Federation in 1901 usually travelled along the former bullock tracks.

Local jealousies caused great transport problems. Different gauges were used when railway tracks were laid in the separate colonies. This caused chaos at state borders when goods and passengers had to be moved to another set of carriages and goods trucks.

There was rejoicing in 1970 when a single gauge railway link opened between Sydney on the east coast and Perth on the western shoreline. Prior to the inaugural run of the new train – called the Indian Pacific as it runs from the Indian Ocean to the Pacific Ocean – passengers and freight had to make four changes of gauge on the trip. The new line cut more than eight hours and over 300 kilometres off the more than 2,500 kilometre journey. As he was about to travel on the first train to run across the nation on a standard gauge line, the Governor General, Sir Paul Hasluck, said: 'This railway is an expression of the fact that we are one nation with common aims and a common destiny'.

Sir Paul said the idea of a standard gauge line across the continent had often been expressed, but it had taken half a century to find the co-operation and economic opportunity to complete it. 'It is a demonstration of our national capacity to undertake great tasks for the good of the nation and to join successfully in great enterprises. It is immediately relevant that this occasion should remind us, and the name Indian Pacific should constantly keep under our notice in the coming years, that Australia's destiny lies in two great oceans, each with its own strategic problems'.

When it was built, the ribbon of steel carrying the new standard gauge rolling stock across the continent passed close by a dusty, pot-holed track for a considerable distance on the barren Nullarbor Plain; a track masquerading as the Eyre Highway, the only road link between Perth and the eastern states. Today, a new Eyre Highway, running across the Nullarbor from Perth to Adelaide – opened to traffic in September, 1976 – completes the last stage of a programme to upgrade and bitumen seal National Highway One, which runs 10,174 kilometres from Port Hedland in the far northwest, around the west coast and through the southern states, then up the eastern seaboard to Cairns in far north Queensland.

'The old Eyre Highway was the only major road in Australia where a motorist could get lost in a pot-hole and lost in a blinding fog of bulldust at the same time', Mr Geoff Virgo, the South Australian Transport Minister, said at the official opening of the new road link. 'A great many people who crossed the Nullarbor under those conditions regarded it as an adventure, but to a great many more the experience was a nightmare. Indeed, even if the crossing was made safely there was no guarantee the vehicle would be good for anything else afterwards.'

For nearly a century of white settlement Australia was an outpost in the Southern Hemisphere. The only news of happenings in other parts of the world was always months old when the tidings were brought by ships, mostly arriving from England. Often three or four ships would arrive at Australian ports with news and then weeks would go by without any further information. Newspapers carried a page headed 'Shipping' followed by the news they brought.

This isolation ended in 1872 when a single strand of galvanised iron wire, swinging from 40,000 poles between Darwin and Adelaide, gave Australia telegraphic communication with London. In Darwin the Australian communication link was hooked into a submarine cable which had just been laid from Alexandria. It was connected to London.

Since then great strides have been made in communications, both within Australia and with many world cities, and Australia is no longer a lonely land separated by the sea from all the other great landmasses.

The constant advances in transportation and communications and in industry, agriculture and commerce have also countered Australia's geographic isolation and made her a valued partner of the world's leading trading nations. Australia's products now flow quickly to other parts of the world, bypassing routes that were once forbidding and long. London and New York, formerly weeks away, are now no more than an overnight journey by jet aircraft.

From north to south Australia measures 3,100 kilometres and, from east to west, 3,900 kilometres. The country's most northerly point – Cape York – is only 1,000 kilometres from the equator. Modern air transport now makes it possible to spend a morning in a tropical city, in Queensland, and the afternoon skiing in the Australian Alps, in the south-east of New South Wales and north-eastern Victoria.

Water is the country's main problem. The combined annual flow of all Australian rivers is only about half as great as that of the Ganges in India.

The Murray River and its tributaries drain 800,000 square hectares of land. Within this river region lies the bulk of Australia's irrigated land; about 6,240 square kilometres.

The Australian climate was probably more hospitable when the first Aborigines reached Australia. The rainfall was heavier and more reliable and today's arid areas, particularly in central Australia, were fertile and well stocked with game. As time went by, and the climate became more arid, the Aborigines sought new hunting areas near coastal centres but never completely deserted the country's interior.

Isolated as the Aborigines were for thousands of years, it is understandable that the earliest European mariners to visit the Australian coastline did not understand them. The colourful English pirate, William Dampier, not only described the Aborigines he saw on the Australian west coast as the 'most miserablest people in the world' but was equally unimpressed with the landscape which he described as 'barren, sandy and destitute of water'. It must have come as a surprise to these European mariners to find human beings in a land about which Europeans had for centuries theorised.

Despite ridicule and sometimes persecution, many theorists stuck to their belief that the world was round and not flat. As their theories gained acceptance, maps appeared inscribed in Latin which referred to *Terra Australis Incognita*.

Portuguese mariners, encouraged by Prince Henry, who became known as Henry the Navigator, overcame suspicion and fear in the 1600s and ventured south until they rounded the southern tip of Africa. They called it the Cape of Storms, though later it became known as the Cape of Good Hope.

Some historians have suggested that the Portuguese may have discovered parts of the Australian coast before 1542 and there have also been suggestions that the Arabs – who were great travellers – may have looked at the Australian coastline earlier than this time. However, it is accepted that coastal exploration of Australia began with the Spaniards and the Dutch in the 1600s and that they were not overly impressed with the land they called New Holland.

Dampier made his first appearance in 1688 and returned in 1699. On his return to England he presented his views on the natives and the countryside and provided descriptions of trees, birds, flowers and reptiles.

Earlier, the Dutch explorer Abel Tasman, sailing from Mauritius, had voyaged through the Roaring Forties until he sighted the rugged coast of southwest Tasmania, which he annexed for Holland and called Van Diemen's Land.

By the end of the 17th century, Europeans still did not know whether Van Diemen's Land and New Zealand were parts of New Holland or whether they were separated from it and formed part of the great Antarctic continent.

It was left to Captain Cook to sail along Australia's eastern shoreline in 1770 and claim ownership for the British Sovereign, George the Third.

Few Australians realise that February 15, 1768 is an important date in their country's history. On that day, the Royal Society in London addressed a Memorial to King George the Third, reminding His Majesty that the planet Venus was due to cross the face of the sun on June 3, 1769 and that if this event was observed and timed accurately, astronomers would be able to calculate the distance between the earth and the sun. One of the points from which the Society considered the transit should be observed was in the South Seas; perhaps one of the Marquesas Group discovered by the Spaniard Mendana or one of the islands of present day Tonga, discovered by Abel Tasman. His Majesty was a keen astronomer but, more pragmatically, his Ministers believed that somewhere south of the equator must lie a southern continent. The advantages of finding this and annexing it for Britain would be valuable in promoting trade and providing naval bases in the Pacific. The Royal Society provided £4,000 sterling and the government agreed to provide a ship for a voyage to the South Seas with a proviso that after the transit of Venus had been observed the ship should make another search for the elusive Great South Land.

The man selected to lead the expedition was James Cook, aged 39. He had risen from the ranks and, although still holding only the non-commissioned rank of Master, had distinguished himself as a navigator, marine surveyor, map maker, astronomer and practical seaman.

On May 25, 1768 he was commissioned lieutenant and two days later the farm labourer's son took command of the ship *Endeavour* to supervise her refitting. He sailed for the South Seas with secret orders only to be opened after the transit of Venus had been observed. The observation took place on June 3, 1769. When he opened the Admiralty's secret orders, Cook found he was instructed to sail to latitude 40 degrees south and to make a thorough search in that vicinity for a continent. If none was found he was to turn west to locate and examine New Zealand, which Tasman had discovered in 1642.

All Cook found was an expanse of grey, turbulent ocean 'peopled' only by sea birds, porpoises and seals. On October 7 he sighted New Zealand and in the next six months circumnavigated both the main islands. He then sailed west but southerly gales prevented the *Endeavour* from reaching Van Diemen's Land and when land was sighted on April 19, 1770 it was the southeast coast of a mainland – today it is part of the State of Victoria. Cook called the spot Point Hicks after his Second Lieutenant, who was the officer on watch when land was sighted.

The *Endeavour* then sailed north and on April 28 was off the entrance to a large bay which looked to be well sheltered. By early afternoon the *Endeavour* was in the bay and at anchor. Aborigines were sighted fishing, but they took little notice of the arrival of the *Endeavour*. However, when Cook and some of his crew went ashore in boats a young man and an older Aboriginal appeared carrying spears. They shouted and waved angrily for them to go away. When the white men landed the Aboriginals hurled spears and it was not until one of them was hit in the leg by a bullet that they fled.

The *Endeavour* stayed eight days. The botanist on board, Sir Joseph Banks, later described the Aborigines as 'lean and nimble with thick bushy hair and beards. They were naked and wore no ornaments and appeared to live in small groups probably of families rather than in a community. They were certainly not Polynesian or Negro'.

When the *Endeavour* put to sea Cook saw the entrance to another harbour a few kilometres north and in his log he recorded that it might provide a safe anchorage; how right he was. Today, Sydney Harbour is world famous and has Sydney, site of the first white settlement in 1788, on its shores.

As the *Endeavour* continued northward, Cook spent much time at the masthead studying the coast which he described as 'diversified' with an agreeable variety of hills and ridges, valleys and large plains all clothed in wood. Banks reported that it had 'shows of fertility'. Today it is one of the richest dairying areas in Australia.

It was while they were off what is today the city of Cairns in Australia's far north that Cook encountered the dangers of the Great Barrier Reef. Great care had to be taken as he made his way through seas increasingly strewn with small islands, rocks and reefs. On the night of January 10, the *Endeavour* ran hard aground on a reef. When she was eventually freed, Cook made for the coast where repairs were made. He then returned to England.

Cook did not agree with the assessments Dampier had made of the Australian countryside and the Aborigines. He said the countryside was not 'barren and miserable' as Dampier had described the western coast. He said '...we find all such things as nature had bestowed upon it in a flourishing state'. He said he believed most sources of grain, fruit, roots etc. would flourish if they 'were brought hither, planted and cultivated by the hand of industry and here are more provision for more cattle at all seasons of the year...'

White settlement began 18 years later, but not because it was a land of great expectations. The loss of the American colonies in the War of Independence had made it necessary for the British to find a new dumping ground for the convicts who were overcrowding their gaols in the unsettled periods of the 18th century.

Sir Joseph Banks, the botanist who had accompanied Captain Cook, had not been overenthusiastic about Australia when he returned to England. However, supported by others who had travelled with Cook, he suggested to the House of Commons that Botany Bay – where the Cook party had spent a week – was ideally situated for a convict settlement. It was far enough away to make it difficult for the convicts to escape and sufficiently fertile to support them.

The first governor, Captain Phillip, did not agree when he reached Botany Bay in 1788 with the First Fleet and more than 1,000 convicts. He decided that it was unsuitable as a settlement and set off with crews in three open boats to explore the harbour a few kilometres north that Captain Cook had named Port Jackson. He was delighted with the harbour, which he described as 'the finest harbour in the world in which a thousand sail of the line may ride in perfect security...' He planted a flag at Sydney Cove and took possession of the land from Cape York in the north of Australia to Van Diemen's Land (Tasmania) in the south, as well as many kilometres of land to the west of Sydney, in the name of the British Crown.

On February 7, 1788 the official document appointing the Governor and establishing court subjugature were read to assembled members of the expedition and the Colony of New South Wales was officially established.

A constant worry for Captain Phillip was how to provide enough food to keep the colonists alive. At the time of settlement the Sydney area was heavily wooded and the colonists lacked livestock to draw their ploughs. They had axes and hoes, but these were not good enough to clear and prepare the land for sowing. Much of the seed brought from England had deteriorated during transit. Another problem was that the convicts, and the marines who had been brought to guard them, knew little about farming.

Fresh water was scarce, and coarse grass and wild animals soon killed the few sheep they had brought with them. They had also brought a herd of cattle, but they soon wandered into the bush and were not sighted till years later, by which time – to the surprise of the settlers – they had grown into several herds and were grazing on rich land now called The Cowpastures, near Camden, west of Sydney. This was the spot where John Macarthur, one of the fathers of the Australian merino sheep industry, established his first flock.

The early European settlers also had problems with the Australian soil. Crop failures, declining yields over the years, and erosion, often caused by poor farming practices, caused a scarcity of fresh food. Slowly, through trial and error, the settlers learned to recognise the best soils of the country and the second half of the 19th century saw great improvements in agricultural production.

Arid inland areas were explored and extensive sheep and cattle stations established. The southern wheatlands were cleared of their native vegetation and irrigation areas were established along the Murray River.

This era also saw a rapid expansion in science and technology in Europe and America. Discoveries in chemistry, physics and biology made possible a host of new industrial products and they provided a basis for the solution to many of Australia's agricultural problems.

Thanks to studies of the soil, particularly in Russia and America, methods of classifying and mapping soil and combating erosion were developed. These discoveries came just in time for Australian agriculture, where yields of wheat were declining in many areas due mainly to a phosphorous deficiency. The answer was superphosphate. Later, poor crop and animal growth in some areas was found to be due to a lack of trace elements – manganese, cobalt, copper, zinc and molybdenum – in the various soils.

Legumes suited to different soil types and climatic conditions were developed and are widely used today under the guidance of the largest research organisation in Australia, the Commonwealth Scientific and Industrial Research Organisation (CSIRO). CSIRO has five research institutes: animal and food science, biological resources, energy and earth resources, industrial technology and physical sciences. The CSIRO's Division of Soils believes that Australia is wealthy enough to be able to get a living from its soil and still conserve it and improve it for future generations.

For 80 years after the arrival of the First Fleet, Britain continued to send convicts to Australia, although transportation to New South Wales ended in 1840 and the State of Victoria, for a long time known as the Port Phillip district, refused to accept them at all. Transportation lingered on in Tasmania until 1853 and ended in Western Australia in 1868.

By that time more than 160,000 convicts had been transported to the Australian colonies, of whom 80,000 went to New South Wales. The convicts faced harsh discipline and hangings were common, particularly for stealing food in the early days of settlement when rationing was necessary for survival.

Today, at least half a million Australians are descendants of the convicts. This once caused anguish to the descendants mixing with free settlers but, today, in Australia's cosmopolitan society it is often a source of pride.

As settlement spread, assigned convicts were often driven up country like herds of cattle, carrying heavy packs up to 50 kilometres a day until they reached their masters' properties.

Others were sent to the penal settlement established at Norfolk Island, 1,670 kilometres from Sydney. This convict settlement quickly earned a reputation for inhumane treatment. Many convicts deliberately committed a 'major' crime, for which the penalty was death, so that they could be hanged rather than remain prisoners on the island. One of the early Governors of New South Wales, Sir Ralph Darling, once said of the Norfolk Island penal colony: 'My object was to hold out that settlement as a place of the extremest punishment short of death'.

The Norfolk Island penal settlement was closed in 1856 to become a new home for the descendants of the *Bounty* mutineers who had remained at Pitcairn Island after they had put the *Bounty*'s Master, Captain Bligh, and other sailors adrift in an open boat, in which they made an epic voyage back to civilisation. Today, Norfolk Island is an external territory controlled by the Australian Federal Government and has become a popular tourist centre.

The first free settlers arrived in Sydney in 1793, at first in a trickle and then at regular intervals, until the gold rushes in New South Wales and Victoria in the 1850s caused a massive inflow of people from many lands.

The early free settlers were mostly English, Irish and Scottish. The discovery of tin brought miners from Cornwall, England, to work the deposits in South Australia; a small group of Italians established themselves in Western Australia and a few Frenchmen arrived with knowledge of wine making. American River on Kangaroo Island, off the South Australian coast, got its name from the homeland of the sealers who used it as a base.

Italians became one of the predominant ethnic groups among the orchards and vineyards along the Murray and Murrumbidgee Rivers' irrigation areas, the sugar plantations of northern Queensland and the tobacco fields in Victoria's Ovens Valley. Greek citizens also settled in the irrigation areas near Mildura in Victoria and Renmark in South Australia.

By the mid-19th century Australia's interior had Afghan camel drivers and in Queensland a kind of slavery developed when South Sea Islanders, known as Kanakas, were herded into the state to be indentured as cheap labour to work the cane fields.

However, it was the gold rushes of the 1850s that really swelled the population. Fortune hunters came from all parts of the globe and the human avalanche often caused turmoil. The Victorian diggings alone attracted more than 40,000 Chinese and on some fields they outnumbered Caucasians. Clashes soon developed between the white men and the Chinese with the latter, who were mostly diligent and hard-working, being brutally treated.

Since then migration to Australia has continued unabated, although there were two periods, from 1898 to 1906 and 1930 to 1932 – perhaps as a result of droughts, economic depressions and their aftermaths – when departures exceeded the Australian intake by more than 50,000.

The post World War Two migration wave changed the culture and the eating habits of the Australian community. The new immigrants brought with them new tastes, new celebrations and new types of festivals. Today Melbourne, the capital of Victoria, has a larger Greek population than any city in Greece apart from Athens. It is commonplace, not only in the Australian cities but in the suburbs and the rural areas as well, to find restaurants serving foods regarded as delicacies in many lands.

Australians did not always accept a cosmopolitan way of life. The flood of Chinese citizens during the gold rush days and the use of Kanakas as slave labour aroused fears that living standards would be reduced. One of the first enactments of the Federal Government when the colonies united as one nation in 1901 was the Immigration Restriction Act, which became known as the 'White Australia' policy. This allowed the Commonwealth of Australia to refuse admission to unwanted migrants. In reality, the aim was to prevent Asian and coloured migrants from becoming permanent residents. Under the Act 'undesirables' could be asked to undergo a dictation test in a European language; the authorities always selected a language which would ensure the applicant's inability to pass the test.

In 1960, the 'White Australia' policy was softened with specific mention of Asians 'being forbidden permanent residence' being dropped. Later the wording was again changed, saying preference would be given to European migrants who would be able to integrate readily. This too has been deleted. Until 1975, British subjects had automatic right of entry into Australia. A new immigration policy was then introduced which applied uniformly without racial discrimination. To many this was the end of the 'White Australia' policy. Until then non-British immigrants had to fulfil a qualifying period and take an oath of loyalty to the British Crown. During the two World Wars even Australian citizens could be, and were, interned if they had been born in an enemy country.

Australia's immigration policy now reads: 'Eligibility for entry for settlement is restricted to certain family members and fiancees and fiances of Australian residents, to others who possess skills, qualifications, personal or other qualities which represent an economic, social or cultural gain to Australia, and to refugees. The grant of passage assistance is restricted to refugees and skilled workers in demand in Australia'.

When the Commonwealth Parliament was created in 1901 its powers included defence and foreign affairs, post and telegraphs, excise duties, control of interstate and overseas trade and immigration policies. Other matters such as divorce, taxation, insurance and banking were also placed within the jurisdiction of the Commonwealth Parliament, but on these matters both the Commonwealth and the State parliaments legislated. In 1911 the State of South Australia transferred the Northern Territory to the Commonwealth.

As a commonwealth, Australia began to prosper. Before World War Two it depended heavily on wool, wheat, meat and dairy products and in the mining industry on gold and lead. Since World War Two there have been great strides in the manufacturing industry and, in a census in 1961, Australian factory workers were shown to outnumber workers in primary industries by four to one. Despite this comparison, primary industry has increased its output and efficiency and still contributes much to the nation's exports.

Most of the state capitals were established as ports and administrative centres and became the focal points of transport, with roads and railways being centred on them.

Australians were well aware, long before a recent Prime Minister, Mr Malcolm Fraser, uttered the words 'that life was not meant to be easy'. Australia has certainly gone through several crises since Federation in 1901. Australia then became a nation of six federated states which, together with the Australian Capital Territory and the Northern Territory, constituted the Commonwealth of Australia. Australia is freely associated with many other countries as a member of the British Commonwealth of Nations.

The states have two levels of government: a state government with residual powers centred on the capital city of the state, and local government authorities with powers based on a State Act of Parliament.

The senior representative of the Monarch in Australia is the Governor-General. Until 1926 he was appointed by the Crown on the advice of the British Parliament. They are now selected on the recommendation of the Australian Federal Government.

The first Governor-General of Australia was the Earl of Hopetoun. He did not make a good start when he invited the Premier of New South Wales, Sir William Lyne – because he represented the senior State – to become the first Prime Minister. Lyne could not get enough support to form a government. Sir Edmund Barton, also from New South Wales, who had played a prominent part in the Federation of the Australian colonies, was then commissioned to form a ministry and on January 1, 1901 became Australia's first Prime Minister.

The first Federal Parliament had three parties: the Protectionists, the Free Traders and the Australian Labor Party, with Labor holding the balance of power.

Barton, a lawyer, was first elected to the New South Wales Legislative Assembly in 1879. He became leader of the movement for Federation and, in 1891, was one of the four men chosen to draft the Constitution Bill. Barton resigned in 1903 to take a seat on the bench of the newly established High Court where, for 17 years, he maintained a reputation as a learned and able judge. His reputation as a national leader was unchallenged. The nation's longest serving Prime Minister, Sir Robert Menzies, once wrote: 'It was indeed a happy thing for Australia that as she grew into united nationhood...she should have been served by so lofty a soul and so single-minded a patriot as Edmund Barton'.

Although the establishment of the Commonwealth on January 1, 1901, is often given the honour of being the date on which Australia achieved nationhood, the honour is often challanged.

Some historians claim nationhood was achieved at the Eureka Stockade insurrection in 1854 in which at least 30 miners, troopers and police lost their lives in a clash on the Ballarat goldfields. Eureka certainly achieved much. It paved the way for the use of the secret ballot and many believe it hastened the granting of manhood suffrage, a review of the land laws enabling ordinary citizens to acquire land, and the creation in Victoria of a two-chamber parliament which, in effect, was self-government.

However, one popular belief is that nationhood was earned on the beaches of Gallipoli in 1915 when valiant Australian troops, together with those of her sister nation, New Zealand, fought as the ANZACs against impossible odds in the ill-fated World War One campaign in Turkey. The word Anzac is based upon the initials of the Australian and New Zealand Army Corps. It is said to have had its origin at the headquarters of the two countries' armed forces in Cairo in 1915 when the corridor outside the Clerk's Room became filled with boxes bearing the words 'Australian and New Zealand Army Corps'.

When a code name was needed for the Corps, the term ANZAC was suggested and the commander, General William Riddell Birdwood, approved. General Birdwood was a British officer born at Kirkee, India, in 1865 and commissioned into the British Army in 1885. He was on Lord Kitchener's staff during the Boer War and also in India. In 1914 he was appointed General Officer Commanding the Australian and New Zealand Army Corps. He directed the Gallipoli campaign and later the British Fifth Army which included the ANZACs.

The name Anzac was given to the cove where the Australians and New Zealanders landed at Gallipoli on April 25, 1915. On that date each year, remembrance ceremonies in Australia and New Zealand honour all those who took part in the operation. The word Anzac now applies in a wider sense to all the Australian and New Zealand servicemen who fought in the 1914-18 War.

The word Anzac has been protected by parliamentary legislation and neither it, or any word resembling it, may be used either commercially or as a title except by permission of the Governor General. It is similarly protected by law in New Zealand and the United Kingdom.

In Canberra, the Federal Capital, the Australian War Memorial is a shrine to the nation's war dead. It has three functions – commemoration, exhibition and the supply of information through its library.

The focal point of the Hall of Memory is a 5.5-metre sculpture of a soldier. On three sides are windows bearing figures of the three fighting services and women's services. In cloisters nearby, a roll of honour lists the dead alphabetically, by service and unit, without rank or decoration or other distinction. The memorial is also an art gallery with a collection of 12,000 works. The museum there contains artefacts from the First Sudan War of 1885 to the Vietnam conflict. The memorial houses more than 3,500,000 items and each year has more than 800,000 visitors. It has been described as the world's 'only real war memorial'.

The Memorial includes the largest collection of Victoria Crosses – 28 – in the Hall of Valour. Each was donated to the Memorial. The V.C. – all of which are cast from a cannon captured during the Crimean War – has been won by 96 Australians fighting in campaigns from the Boer War to Vietnam.

Each Anzac Day the Governor-General takes the salute at the national ceremony. In Victoria, Melbourne has its Shrine of Remembrance which is somewhat like the design of an ancient Egyptian or Inca pyramid. Dedicated in 1934 – the centenary year of white settlement in the state – the shrine was built so that marchers in the annual Anzac Day parade can see it every step of the way. An aperture in the ceiling of the inner sanctuary allows a ray of light to fall on the Rock of Remembrance at precisely the eleventh hour of the eleventh day of the eleventh month – Armistice Day.

General Birdwood, who had commanded the Anzacs, was keen to become the Governor General of Australia in 1931 but the Prime Minister, Mr James Scullin, insisted that an Australian get the appointment for the first time, and the honour went to a distinguished scholar and jurist, Sir Isaac Isaacs. Birdwood was appointed Master of Peterhouse at Cambridge University and was granted a peerage as First Baron of Anzac and Totnes in 1938. He died in 1951.

An Australian historian, Professor Russel Ward, has written: 'If Australia was born at Gallipoli she came of age at Singapore'. In the Second World War, the fall of Singapore to the Japanese in 1942 left Australia on her own for the first time in her history to organise her own defence. No longer could she rely on Britain, the Mother Country, to come to her aid. She was too busy fighting for her own survival.

The Australian Prime Minister of that time, Mr John Curtin, faced the challenge with great courage. He refused to accede to a request by the great British wartime leader, Sir Winston Churchill, to transfer Australian troops – who had been serving in the Middle East – to a new war front in Burma. Australia had already lost a division of troops – the 8th – with the fall of Singapore and Malaya.

Australia needed help and Mr Curtin turned to the United States. As he did, he declared: 'Without inhibitions of any kind I make it quite clear that Australia looks to America free of any pangs as to our traditional links or kinship with the United Kingdom. We know the problems with which the United Kingdom is faced. We know too that Australia can go and Britain can still hold on. We are therefore determined that Australia shall not go and we shall exert all our energy towards shaping our plans with the United States as its keynote which will give our country some confidence of being able to hold out until the tide of battle turns against the enemy'.

Mr Curtin invited the American General Douglas MacArthur to Australia and when he came, gave him freedom to convert the whole continent as a base for the gigantic combined force required for the task of driving back the Japanese.

The Curtin Government's declaration changed the course of this island continent's history. When Mr Curtin was in London in 1944 attending a gathering of Prime Ministers, Sir Winston – despite the fact that he had differed sharply with Curtin over the recall of the Australian troops from the Middle East – told the assemblage: 'This most commanding, competent and whole-hearted leader of the Australian people in their vicissitudes, terrors and mortal perils through which they have passed, has made a great impression on all who have come in contact with him'.

Curtin also showed great strength on another issue, which he had opposed in World War One – conscription. The Curtin Government introduced conscription not only for industry but also for the armed forces in World War Two. The great strain of the war years took its toll and Curtin died in office in 1945.

Australia had come a long way since that fine, cloudless day on January 26, 1788, when the British flag was hoisted at Sydney Cove and Captain Arthur Phillip took possession of New South Wales in the name of the British Crown.

However, it was not the first time that Australia – for a century nervous of the possible expansionary moves south by Asian countries, particularly Japan – had looked to the United States. In 1902, Australians were well aware of the need for a close relationship with America. One of the nation's leading morning newspapers, *The Sydney Morning Herald*, in an editorial of 1902 said: 'It is likely that the United States will be our first line of defence against Asia'.

The British Government was not happy when the three times Australian Prime Minister, Mr Alfred Deakin, issued an invitation to the United States Fleet to visit Australia. Deakin did not bother to consult the 'Mother Country'.

Although he had been elected Prime Minister, Mr Deakin continued his craft of journalism and contributed articles to the *London Morning Post* under a pseudonym. On a possibility of a visit by the U.S. Fleet he wrote: 'We have never seen a single British battleship in these waters and the prospect of 16 of them (American) in Port Jackson (Sydney Harbour)...may well awaken fresh emotions'. On August 28, 1908, the Great White Fleet entered Sydney Harbour to a tremendous welcome, which prompted Mr Deakin to refer to 'The strength of the invisible ties drawing us together as States united in affection'.

In 1951 Australia, New Zealand and the United States signed a defence treaty called the Anzus Pact, which provides for mutual aid and co-operative action in the event of an armed attack on any of the member countries, their island protectorates, armed forces, aircraft or vessels in the Pacific. Later agreements between Australia and the United States have enabled the Americans to establish military and communications stations at North West Cape in Western Australia and Pine Gap in the Northern Territory.

The actual date that Australia reached nationhood does not matter; only the fact that it has been reached. In recent years there has been a growing demand to make Australia Day – celebrated on January 26 – one that celebrates more than the arrival of Captain Arthur Phillip and his shiploads of convicts, because it is a cause for national pride and unity.

In an Australia Day message on January 26, 1984, the Prime Minister, Mr Bob Hawke said: 'Australia is a nation of many different influences. From the first Aboriginals to the most recent settlers, people from all over the world have contributed to our exciting and colourful heritage. It is important that as a nation we preserve and enhance the best of these influences for all to share. Australia Day is the occasion for us all to pause and reflect upon what it is that we wish to pass on to future generations'.E
When they landed in 1788, the First Fleeters pitched their tents at Sydney Cove which, today, has one of the world's most controversial 'masterpieces' sited on it. It is the Sydney Opera House, with its roofs depicting billowing white sails, and it is easily Australia's chief tourist attraction.

Less than a kilometre away is another masterpiece – the Sydney Harbour Bridge – which provides a further reminder of the progress the city, the State of New South Wales and the nation of Australia have made in less than two centuries. The bridge is famous for its single span; not the longest in the world but the most massive. The main span is 503 metres long with the top of the arch 134 metres above sea level.

Looking over its masterpieces is the City of Sydney with its towering skyscrapers, and on both sides of the harbour is a sprawling suburbia which stretches 70 kilometres from north to south and for 55 kilometres from the inland west to the Pacific Ocean. More than three million people live in Sydney, the capital of a state which has more than five million of the nation's 15 million-plus population.

The state has a fertile coastal strip, some of the best pastoral land in Australia and 1,900 kilometres of Pacific Ocean shoreline which has become a holiday paradise with its many white-sanded beaches, tranquil inlets and rocky headlands. It has many beauty spots: not only Sydney Harbour, but the Blue Mountains, the Jenolan and other limestone caves and several forests and parks which are home to much of Australia's animal life.

New South Wales also has the Snowy Mountains; a holiday retreat in winter for skiers and famous for its Alpine wildflowers which carpet the slopes and high plains in the summer.

The Snowys have Australia's highest peak, Mt Kosciusko, and for 25 years it became the United Nations area of Australia when men from many nations built the country's largest single engineering project – the $800 million Snowy Mountains Hydro-Electric Scheme. Using 16 dams and 134 kilometres of tunnels, the waters from the Snowy feed seven power stations capable of generating 3.7 million kilowatts of electricity for southeastern Australia.

New South Wales is also a state of boundless plains which sweep away into the western haze; a land of sheep and cattle pastures, fields of ripening wheat, irrigation channels, vineyards and orchards and tree-lined mountain slopes. As the original state of Australia, it has much to remind citizens of the toil and sweat of the pioneers who erected buildings that are today historic.

Apart from Sydney, the state has many cities and towns, including two steel and coal cities north and south of Sydney: Newcastle in the north and Wollongong in the south.

The state's tourist books claim that almost every city, town and village has attractions individual in character set against a vast, unifying landscape and that with an overall area of 801,600 square kilometres the countryside changes by the kilometre.

The many inland cities include Bathurst which, as a small town, was close to the site where payable gold was first found, starting off the gold rush days of the 1850s. Tamworth is the country music centre of Australia; Bourke, in the state's far west, is regarded as the 'gateway to the real outback'; Albury is a southern border town on the Murray River and was once called the 'crossing place' – this was an area used by the early settlers to spread settlement over the river into Victoria – and, of course, Broken Hill, the 'silver city' which became the world's largest and richest supplier of silver, lead and zinc. This outback community claims it has contributed more to Australia's industrial development than any other district. It certainly provided the impetus to transform the nation from a pastoral land into one of the most industrialised nations in the Southern Hemisphere. It is also different from any other Australian city. In its centenary year brochure in 1983 it described itself as 'another world – right here in Australia'.

New South Wales was also once the world's main producer of tin and, today, its mainstays of industry are the huge basins of high quality black coal found by the pioneers soon after white settlement began.

The Colony of New South Wales in its early years was limited to an area surrounding Sydney. Expansion to the west was blocked by a barrier of mountains – now known as the Blue Mountains – and the countryside to the north and south was criss-crossed with fast-flowing rivers which were a danger to any who attempted to cross them.

Australia's first farmer was an ex-convict called James Ruse and he was soon followed by other emancipists, soldiers and non-commissioned officers of the Marine Corps who were given land when their period of service ended. By the time the first free settlers arrived in 1793 there were nearly 200 farms around Sydney and explorers were slowly ranging up and down the coast.

The colony had about 4,000 residents, including the convicts at Norfolk Island, when Governor Phillip returned to England in 1792. For the next 18 years various governors – like Phillip, former naval officers – battled with limited success to solve the problems of the colony.

A major problem was the inability of the governors to control the special army corps which had been raised in England to replace the First Fleet marines. The first detachment of the new corps, which reached Sydney in 1790, was destined to be dubbed the 'Rum Corps', and to play an energetic and inglorious role in the colony's history.

They so exasperated one of the early governors, Captain John Hunter, that he described the corps as 'Soldiers from the Savoy (a British military prison of the day) and other characters who have been considered disgraceful in their regiments in His Majesty's Service'.

During the three years between the change of the first two governors – Phillip and Hunter – the corps commander, Major Grose, and his second in command were in charge of the colony. With no governor in the colony, the corps officers were given priority in the selection of land. The Corps raised enough money to send a ship to Cape Town seeking provisions. As well as returning with food, the ship carried large stocks of spirits. Soon the officers of the corps had established a regular and prosperous trade in rum.

One member of the corps was the sheepman Lieutenant John Macarthur, who spent many of his years in Australia not only developing the merino sheep industry and in politics, but quarrelling with the various governors.

The corps proved too much for Governor Hunter, who was replaced by Governor Philip Ridley King, and he soon clashed with Macarthur. He called him a 'perturbator' and wrote of him 'experience has convinced every man in the Colony there are no resources which cunning, impudence and a pair of basilisk eyes can afford that he does not put into practice'.

After one clash, Macarthur and fellow officers boycotted the Governor's residence and when the Corp's then Commanding Officer, William Paterson, refused to join the boycott, Macarthur disclosed the contents of a letter that Paterson's wife had sent to Macarthur's wife. Deeply upset, Paterson challenged Macarthur to a duel in which Paterson was wounded. Macarthur was sent to England to face a court martial, but it was abandoned for lack of witnesses and Governor King was admonished.

Macarthur took the opportunity in England to discuss wool-growing prospects in New South Wales. It was the start of the great Australian wool industry.

Macarthur soon clashed with the new governor, William Bligh, of *HMS Bounty* fame, when he returned to Sydney and assisted the Rum Corps in deposing the governor in 1808. The Corps rushed to Macarthur's aid when the governor charged him with treason. Later Bligh, back in England, was exonerated of charges that he had subverted the laws of the colony. In 1809, Macarthur was again in England and his only punishment for the part he had played in having Bligh deposed was 'temporary exile' from the colony.

Macarthur continued to disagree with governors and to take a leading part in many community projects. He died in 1834. Despite his temperament and inability to get on with the governors, Macarthur, ably assisted by his wife Elizabeth, did much to shape the early history of the colony and although he may not have actually fathered the merino wool industry, his services and those of his sons in developing, publicising and improving the quality of the early fleeces were decisive features in the nation's rural history.

The rule of the Rum Corps ended in 1810 when an army officer, Colonel Lachlan Macquarie, was appointed Governor of the Colony, and arrived with his own regiment. The colony made great headway under Governor Macquarie – morals improved and exploration was encouraged. The latter led to the crossing of the Blue Mountains in 1813 by Wentworth, Blaxland and Lawson and opened up the rich pastures of the western plains.

A serious problem in the early days of settlement was the imbalance of the sexes; men outnumbered women by ten to one. By 1806, 50 per cent of all children born in the colony were illegitimate.

Governor Macquarie encouraged emancipists to take up farming and he used a convict architect named Francis Greenaway, who was to change the shape of Sydney's skyline.

But Macquarie's emancipist policies were not approved of by many of the free settlers and a special investigator named John Blegge – sent to Sydney by the British Government – agreed with the free settlers. Macquarie resigned and left the colony.

Agitation for self-government began in the 1820s and one of its proponents was William Charles Wentworth of Blue Mountains crossing fame. Wentworth, a lawyer, began to devote all of his time to political and pastoral interests and, with the support of most of the colonists, pressed for self-government.

The other big issue at the time was transportation of convicts. When they stopped coming to New South Wales in 1840, it was the result of English pressure rather than that from New South Wales colonists.

During this time the inland march of settlement began, as did the era of the squatter (an illegal landowner). They soon occupied big areas of the Western plains. The squatters did their own exploring and official parties of explorers were often surprised when they entered supposedly unexplored land to find white men already in residence. The squatters defied Government attempts to confine them to certain areas and one governor, Sir Richard Bourke, decided squatting could not be prevented and granted pastoral leases. The sheep flocks increased rapidly and by 1880 Australia had become the world's leading woolgrower.

By 1836 most of the Australian states had been created, although Victoria – known as the Port Phillip District – and Queensland still came under the control of New South Wales. Victoria was created a separate colony in 1851 and Queensland in 1859.

The 1850s brought self-government and the first announced discovery of gold, which caused frenzied activity as migrants from many parts of the world poured into the country to seek their fortunes. Gold had, in fact, been found in New South Wales in 1823, but it was not announced because there were fears it could cause uprisings among the convicts and wreck the quiet expansion of the colony.

The New South Wales gold announcement made such an impact that the rush to the diggings forced the Victorian Government to set up a Gold Discovery Committee and offer a reward of £200 ($400) for a payable gold find within 320 kilometres of Melbourne.

In June 1851, gold was found at Clunes in Victoria, followed quickly by many other finds, and within three years the population of Victoria had quadrupled. Gold was soon found in all the other Australian Colonies. It brought its riches but it also caused social problems, including the resentment of the white diggers against the Chinese immigrants.

But a bigger problem was the wrath of the diggers over payment for gold licences and what they claimed was the oppressive treatment handed out by the troopers.

In Victoria the miners formed the Ballarat Reform League, which sought to have the licence fees abolished and the end of the system whereby members of the Government's Legislative Council (Upper House) had to be landowners.

When their demands were ignored, the miners burned their licences in a huge bonfire and elected an Irishman named Peter Lalor as their leader. On December 3, 1854 a stockade built by the miners was attacked by troopers and police and in a short time about 30 people from both sides were dead. About 120 miners were taken prisoner and their leaders put on trial, but no jury would convict them.

Of Eureka, famous American author Mark Twain, who spent some time in Australia, wrote in his *More Tramps Abroad* that it was 'the finest thing in Australian history...it was the Barons and John over again...it was Concord and Lexington...another instance of victory won by a lost battle'.

Eureka was not Australia's first rebellion. This occurred at Castle Hill, now a suburb of Sydney, when Irish convicts rose in revolt against their treatment. Unrest had been rife among Irish prisoners for some years. All was quiet in the Castle Hill convict quarters throughout the day on Sunday, March 4, 1804. But, at about 8 p.m. 200 convicts assembled, rang the prison bell, set a house on fire and began a search for arms. Led by Philip Cunningham, a stonemason and ex-soldier, they broke out of their quarters, but before doing so they dragged Robert Duggan, the official flogger, from under a bed and gave him a taste of his own whip.

The convict plan was to gain the help of convicts in other areas in the district and set up a 'Liberty Pole' in front of Government House in Parramatta; also a suburb of Sydney today. They then planned to march on Sydney, seize ships in the harbour and escape.

News of the rising reached Sydney about midnight and the New South Wales Corps and the men of an organisation called the Loyal Association were called out. Cunningham was later taken alive and hanged, as were eight other rebels. Nine received floggings (200 to 500 lashes) and some 50 were sent to a convict settlement in northern New South Wales.

The gold boom did not last long but in its few years of glory Victoria produced more gold than any other Australian state. The gold 'riches' also attracted the villains and bushrangers, who had been reported as far back as 1805 when the *Sydney Gazette* said that a cart had been stopped by three men 'whose appearance sanctioned the suspicion of their being bushrangers'.

The British investigator John Bigge, in his 1821 report, had defined bushranging as 'absconding in the woods and living upon plunder and the robbery of orchards'. In 1835 Charles Darwin said 'a bushranger is an open villain who subsists by highway robbery and will sooner be killed than taken alive'. Several, like Jack Donahue, Ben Hall and particularly Ned Kelly have become folk heroes.

By the 1830s, bushranging had become so great an evil that the New South Wales Legislative Council passed an Act which, among other things, provided for a suspected person to be apprehended without a warrant; that anyone suspected of having arms might be searched and that police, if provided with general search warrants, could enter or break into any house, seize firearms and arrest the inmates. Convicted robbers and housebreakers were to be condemned to death and executed on the third day thereafter.

Perhaps the best-known bushranger was Ned Kelly who, with his brother Dan and two friends, Joe Byrne and Steve Hart, terrorised communities in Victoria and parts of New South Wales and became a police killer. The governments of Victoria and New South Wales put a price of £8,000 (16,000 dollars) on their heads, which was a lot of money in those days.

Dan Kelly, Byrne and Hart died when police trapped them in a hotel at Glenrowan in Victoria. Ned escaped but returned to the scene in a suit of armour to challenge the police. They wounded him in the leg and captured him.

In October, 1880, he was tried for murder, found guilty and was hanged on November 11. Thousands of people stood in silence outside the Melbourne gaol while the death sentence was carried out. Many agreed that Ned's wild career – he was the son of an Irish emancipist – was directed against the injustices of the day, such as colonial repression and the English dislike of the Irish, and were convinced that Ned had been 'hunted like a dog in his native land'.

Tasmania became Australia's second colony in 1825 when it was separated from New South Wales. Australia's smallest state, Tasmania is situated 320 kilometres south of the mainland and is a shield-shaped island about the size of Scotland. It is divided from the mainland by Bass Strait.

Dutch navigator Abel Tasman first sighted the island in 1642 and called it Van Diemen's land in honour of the governor general of the Dutch East Indies. The Dutch paid no further interest in the island. White settlement began in 1803 and soon the island became a British convict centre. When transportation to the island ended in 1852, more than 67,000 convicts had been sent there.

Tasmania has a moist and cool climate and, unlike the mainland, has rarely experienced a drought. Dairying flourishes and it has won world acclaim as the 'Apple Isle'. Most of western Tasmania is inaccessible, with thickly overgrown mountains and gorges. The high centre of the island has many lakes with hydro-electric schemes based on them.

The state capital, Hobart, is on the Derwent River in the south and is Tasmania's largest city. Second largest is Launceston on the Tamar River in the north.

Tasmania has a crumpled terrain and is the world's most mountainous island. Many parts of the island are still unexplored wilderness with a guaranteed high rainfall. Snow can usually be seen in all seasons and central Tasmania experiences freezing temperatures for about 100 days each year.

Tasmania has much beauty, and earned this praise from the English author Anthony Trollope in 1872: 'It is acknowledged by all the rival colonies that of all the colonies Tasmania is the prettiest'.

Not so pretty was the barbaric treatment white men handed out to the island's first inhabitants – the Aborigines. It only took just over 70 years of white settlement to wipe out the island's black inhabitants. The first two decades of white settlement saw the Aborigines killed almost without provocation, chased off their hunting grounds and their huts burnt. In 1830, an attempt was made to save the race – there were then about 200 – but this failed and, in 1876, the last full-blooded Aboriginal, Truganini, died in Hobart aged 73.

The mainland gold rush in the 1850s took most of Tasmania's population but the manpower flow was reversed when a rich tin field was discovered at Waratah, followed by gold strikes at Beaconsfield and copper and silver finds at Mt Lyell and Zeehan.

Perhaps Australia's most famous convict prison is Port Arthur, which is situated on Tasmania's southeastern coast, 96 kilometres from Hobart. Today it is an important tourist attraction. Founded in 1830 during the rule of Lieutenant-Governor George Arthur, the prison was part of a complex of institutions on the Tasman Peninsula. There have been many tales of infamy, and cruel treatment to convicts at Port Arthur; some are true and others are false. There is no doubt that discipline was strict but, according to historians, conditions were better than in many British gaols. Convicts could learn a trade and classes in reading, writing and arithmetic were held nightly after supper. Port Arthur did not have any women convicts.

Tasmania has cashed in on its heritage; it spends, on tourism, more per head than any other Australian state. Tasmania, with a population of just over 400,000 is proud of its native sons and daughters who have achieved fame. They include a prime minister, Joseph Lyons, who was born in a weatherboard house in the small settlement of Stanley in the state's northwest. His wife, Dame Enid Muriel Lyons, was the first woman to be elected to the Federal House of Representatives (Lower House). In 1949 she became Vice-President of the Executive Council and was the first woman to become a Cabinet minister.

Hobart was the birthplace of Hollywood star Errol Flynn, who was the swashbuckling hero of such films as *Captain Blood, The Adventures of Robin Hood* and *The Sea Hawk*. Tasmania was also the birthplace of actress Merle Oberon, pianist Eileen Joyce and Colonel Henry Murray, the most decorated Allied soldier of World War One.

Tasmania may be the prettiest Australian state and the smallest, but one not much bigger – Victoria – is not far behind with its scenic beauty. Although it only occupies three per cent of the mainland landmass, Victoria, known as the 'Garden State', provides a quarter of the nation's rural wealth, 30 per cent of the country's work force and 35 per cent of its manufacturing activity. Victoria is also the envy of other Australian states as it has the nation's best highways and railway network. It also has more than a quarter of Australia's 15 million plus population, 2,700,000 of whom live in the capital, Melbourne. Only New South Wales, which controlled Victoria in the early colonial days, has a bigger population.

The state's climate is decided mainly by the Great Dividing Range, which runs from Northern Queensland down through New South Wales and enters Victoria northeast of the Australian Alps. South of the Divide the weather is cooler and wetter than to the north, but generally the state has four mild seasons. The state's western area has lush, green downs which have earned it the reputation of being the best pasture land in Australia and was described as 'This Eden' by the famous colonial explorer Major Thomas Mitchell, when he surveyed the scene in 1836.

In the early 19th century two attempts to create convict settlements in Victoria failed and, when settlement really got under way in 1834, Victorians refused to accept the shiploads of convicts Britain was sending to other states.

From its early days, when it was controlled by New South Wales, Victorians have defied officialdom. The first settlers came from Tasmania. They were John Batman and John Fawkner and, of course, the first farmers were the Henty brothers who had also crossed, like Batman and Fawkner, without permission, to become farmers in Portland in Victoria's far southwest. Squatters from Tasmania, and soon afterwards from New South Wales, began to cultivate the land and this forced the New South Wales Governor, Sir Richard Bourke, to open up the land. By the 1840s Victorians were calling for separation from New South Wales and this was granted in 1851.

Gold finds caused thousands of immigrants to pour in from many lands. Victoria then enjoyed many years of prosperity and, when the gold production fell to a trickle, most of the miners stayed and tilled the pastures.

For 40 years Melbourne was Australia's most populated city and for a long time was recognised as the financial centre of Australia. Sydney regained the 'biggest city' title early in the 20th century and has had no trouble in retaining it and now also contests Melbourne's claim of being the country's financial centre. But no state has challenged Victoria's 'Garden State' title, or its tourist handout which says: 'From desert to snow, from mountains to the sea, Victoria offers the tourist all that Australia has to offer – Australia in capsule'.

Victoria is probably Australia's most sports-minded state and gave the nation Australian Rules; a game which has no resemblance to any other team sport, except perhaps Gaelic football. Its capital, Melbourne, also has the Melbourne Cup,

the nation's richest horse race which, on the first Tuesday in November each year, is run over 3,200 metres at the beautiful suburban Flemington racecourse. Millions of dollars are staked on the race and it is one day of the year when interstate jealousies are forgotten. It is a race that causes even Federal and State Parliaments to adjourn for a few minutes so that parliamentarians can watch the race on television. Cup day is also a public holiday in Victoria.

Unlike the bigger states, Victoria is not rich in ores, but it does have energy. In Bass Strait oil rigs have produced tonnes of 'black gold' to help Australia reduce its import costs and in its Latrobe Valley are the world's largest deposits of brown coal.

Melbourne likes to be known as a 'fun city' and has the best art gallery in the country. Melbourne's annual Moomba – 'Let's get together and have fun' festival runs for 10 days each March. It is a series of outdoor art shows, band and other concerts, theatrical performances and a giant procession of decorated floats in a colourful Mardi Gras atmosphere.

In 1956 Melbourne was the host city for the Olympic Games, which caused the Prime Minister, Sir Robert Menzies to say: 'In the course of my life I have seen many magnificent sights. I have seen nothing more stirring than the opening and closing days in the main stadium'. These ceremonies were held at the Melbourne Cricket Ground which today can accommodate 120,000 spectators.

Western Australia is known as Australia's 'Wildflower State'. It is also the country's biggest state with an area of 2,525,000 square kilometres, which represents about one-third of the continent. It has more climatic regions and differences than any other state and is so big that it could accommodate most of the other Australian states.

However, for many years after the convict settlement was established in New South Wales in 1788, Britain paid no attention to the western part of New Holland. Western Australia was eventually claimed in 1826 when an outpost was established at King George's Sound on the southwest coast. This became known as Albany. It really was an outpost as, in those days, it was about 3,000 kilometres by sea from the nearest white settlement in Hobart and further away from Sydney. Until 1917, when the trans-continental railway was built, there was no land transport between Western Australia and the rest of the nation. Between Western Australia and the other states is a waterless desert which, at that time, had only seen a few hardy explorers and their camels.

The Aborigines inhabited Western Australia at least 30,000 years ago and the Dutch explorer, Dirck Hartog, is believed to have been the first European to land on its shores in 1616. In the 1600s, Dutch vessels often used the west coast as a landfall and they were followed by the English pirate, William Dampier, who could find nothing good to report about the countryside or the Aborigines.

In 1826, the threat of French possession caused the British to land at Albany and three years later they founded the settlement of Swan, now the capital, Perth.

For years Western Australia was a state without British convicts. They were introduced in 1850 and their arrival boosted the state's economy and population. The convicts built roads and inland development accelerated. Between 1850 and 1868 nearly 10,000 convicts arrived in Western Australia, many of whom were skilled craftsmen. They constructed many fine buildings, some of which remain to this day as monuments to the excellence of the architecture of the Victorian era.

The pastoral industry soon progressed with sheep farmers spreading up the coast, and the introduction of cattle developed a thriving beef industry in the Kimberleys in the north.

However, as with New South Wales and Victoria, it was gold that set the West on the road to prosperity. Gold was found at Halls Creek in 1885 and in other areas, but the real bonanzas were at Coolgardie and Kalgoorlie. The rush to the goldfields pushed Western Australia's population from 35,000 to 239,000 in 20 years and, at one time, the famous Golden Mile at Kalgoorlie produced more than 2,000,000 ounces of gold a year. The rip-roaring gold days faded away as the 20th century began, but the state turned to wheat production, and timber and pearling industries flourished.

Today, Western Australia is Australia's most important mineral state. In the mid-1960s, huge iron ore deposits were opened up at Pilbara and about 100 million tonnes of ore, worth some 1,000 million dollars, are gouged out of huge mines each year and exported from deep-water ports.

Western Australia's mineral wealth has changed Perth from a big town into a city of skyscrapers with a population of more than 800,000. Perth gained world publicity in 1962 when it became known as the 'City of Lights'. The citizens turned on every light possible to provide a 'landmark' for astronaut John Glenn when he made a night-time pass over the city.

Western Australia has more than 7,000 native flower species blossoming in the spring and the countryside is famous for its kaleidoscope of colour. Three-quarters of the species flourish in the state's southwest corner where, protected between the deserts and the oceans, they have been allowed to develop in undisturbed isolation. The splendours of colour and diversity of tint and shade have made this flora world famous.

During the Western Australian winter and spring the burgeoning of this striking natural phenomenon provides an unparalleled display. In May, the first winter rains are enjoyed and then some of the wattles, white heaths and sundews begin to provide splashes of loveliness. As the weeks pass, more and more blossoms ornament what may have been previously disregarded as uninteresting and often dusty growth on shrubs, climbers and trees. More and more annuals thrust up little sprays or long spikes to beautify paddocks, bushes and the roadside.

By October, there is a magnificent showing of flowers of all types and colours, small and large, delicate and handsome. It is a wild garden millions of hectares in extent. Even the long, hot, dry summer is brightened by vast arrays of smokebush, by eucalyptus trees and shrubs in bloom, by verticordias in all their loveliness, and by the many kinds of Banksia and Christmas tree which throw their flaming inflorescence against the cloudless, blue sky.

While much of the general Australian flora has been changed by climatic variations and oceanic submergence, the southwest of Western Australia has remained untouched through aeons. As a result, many genera have evolved in an unchanged habitat and reached a state of development quite different from plant life in other, less tranquil areas.

In the northwest, Western Australia is subject to monsoons and is tropical with a hot, sticky wet season. Further south, the Gibson Desert and the Great Victorian Desert merge into one harsh, empty wasteland. The interior is a dry, empty tableland which is one of the oldest known land areas. It dates back 2,600 million years and has remained virtually unchanged for 1,100 million years. A rock found near Marble Bar is believed to contain the oldest known form of life; the remains of organisms which lived 3,500 million years ago.

The southwest of the state, where most of the population lives, has a Mediterranean-type climate. It also has magnificent forests of karri and jarrah trees which supply the timber industry. It is the edge of a seemingly endless wheat belt that stretches from Esperance in the south to Geralton on the northern coast and grows almost 30 per cent of Australia's crop. There are also sheeplands.

West Australians have always had a feeling of isolation from and neglect by the eastern Australian states and, from time to time, there have been rumblings about secession from the Commonwealth. In 1933, West Australians voted two to one to secede but this was not possible under the Federal Constitution.

One Australian state differs from the others; South Australia. Its first white settlers were all free men and it stayed that way; South Australia has no convict past.

Although sealers established a settlement on Kangaroo Island off the coast in 1804, and famous British navigator Matthew Flinders surveyed the coastline in 1801-02, the first white settlers did not arrive until 1836. The original settlement was under the aegis of the South Australian Association, an organisation formed in London to pioneer the new colony. The first settlers landed at Nepean Bay and Kangaroo Island but, in 1837, a surveyor-general named Colonel William Light arrived with a commission from the Colonisation Committee in London to establish the site for the capital city of the colony.

Against much opposition, including that of the first Governor, Captain John Hindmarsh, Colonel Light selected Adelaide on the Torrens River as the site for the capital. The colonel issued an historic statement which said: 'The reasons that led me to fix Adelaide where it is I do not expect to be generally understood or calmly judged of at present. My enemies, however, by disputing their validity in every particular, have done me the good service of fixing the whole of the responsibility upon me. I am perfectly willing to bear it and I leave it to posterity and not to them to decide whether I am entitled to praise or to blame'. Posterity has certainly praised him.

Adelaide was named after Queen Adelaide, wife of King William IV. Colonel Light planned the city on a grid basis, which provided that the city should comprise the centres of Adelaide and North Adelaide surrounded by parkland areas shaped like a square-cornered figure eight.

The city's early days were troublesome because of its positioning on alluvial mud plains. This meant mud and marshes in winter and dust in summer. But by 1838 the city had been surveyed, with houses and streets being laid out in an orderly fashion.

Today, Adelaide, with a population of more than 900,000, is Australia's fourth largest city. About 70 per cent of South Australians live in the metropolis. Every two years Adelaide holds a Festival of Arts, a cultural occasion which runs for three weeks featuring all the arts: concerts, performances, exhibitions and displays, plus light entertainment, processions and parades.

The state occupies about one-fifth of the continent but much of the countryside is arid. Hovever, thanks to its early European settlers it produces 75 per cent of Australia's wine output and 80 per cent of her brandy, from grapes harvested in the Barossa Valley and nearby grape-growing areas.

It is a flat state; 80 per cent of its area is less than 300 metres above sea level. South Australians have been happy to leave much of its outback a wilderness in order to live in the cooler, hospitable south.

Overall, the state receives less rain than any other, but Adelaide and other southern areas enjoy adequate rainfall, with temperatures ranging from 12 degrees Celsius in July to 23 degrees Celsius in February. The city averages seven hours of sunshine a day.

In the latter part of the 19th century, chief products were wheat, wool, hides, fruit and wine but the 20th century has seen great growth in manufacturing, including motor cars, electrical goods and household appliances.

North of Adelaide, in a desert atmosphere, lies Lake Eyre, on which Donald Campbell, in 1964, sped over the glistening crust of salt to set a world land speed record. The massive lake has rarely been filled with water since it was discovered by explorer John Eyre, in 1840.

The state has Woomera located in its arid centre, which provided Britain and Australia with a base to test guided missiles and for the operation of equipment for international space research programmes. *Woomera* is an Aborigine term for a spear-throwing stick. It was selected in 1947 because of its remoteness, dry climate, clarity of atmospheric conditions and for its availability of an unrestricted area stretching nearly 2,000 kilometres to the northwest.

Mt Gambier, the state's second biggest city, sprawls on the slopes of an extinct volcano which rises 190 metres above the plain.

Every November, one of Australia's mysteries – Blue Lake – situated in a crater, changes colour overnight from grey to sparkling blue and reverts to grey in the Australian autumn. Scientists have no explanation. The area has the Naracoorte Caves where finds of great interest to scientists have been made. They include skeletal remains of long-extinct animals, dead for more than 170,000 years.

The mighty Murray River has a peaceful ending after its long journey from the Snowy Mountains in New South Wales, when it enters Lake Alexandrina and then the sea. Bird life is prolific and it is a popular spot for fishermen. Lake Alexandrina is Australia's largest permanent freshwater lake; it is 40 kilometres long and, in places, almost as wide.

Up the Murray is Riverland, where irrigation has created an oasis, and a fruit industry which produces millions of oranges each year as well as large crops of peaches, apricots and other fruits.

At the first Adelaide City Council meeting each year, the Lord Mayor toasts Colonel William Light as he drinks from an historic loving cup. The citizens are grateful for his genius in providing a city surrounded by parklands.

Queensland – Australia's second largest state – takes up nearly one quarter of the continent. Today it is Australia's fastest growing state, one reason being its relaxed life style and pleasant climate. In 1982 Australia had a population growth rate of 1.60 per cent; Queensland's was 3.32.

Queensland is a state of contrast: it has the Simpson Desert, a desolate, sandy waste, and steaming tropical jungle. It has Australia's wettest town – Tully – and outback hamlets where it might not rain for years. It has sparkling, wave-lapped beaches, which are idyllic holiday playgrounds in the calm months and lashed by storms in the cyclone season. It has forest-clad mountains, their heads hidden in cloud, flat spinifex plains that seem to disappear off the edge of the earth in their vastness, the Wet and the Dry, and the Great Barrier Reef. At Birdsville, in its far west, an annual horse race meeting attracts outback people from hundreds of kilometres away to multiply the normal population of 80 many times over, creating one of the country's most colourful sporting spectacles. The town grew up on the edge of the Simpson Desert a century ago as a centre for moving stock south and as a customs post.

A satellite photograph shows Queensland as a rich, narrow coastal plain in the east backed by the erratic sprawl of the Great Dividing Range. To the west of the ranges stretch vast, dry plains, rising in the northwest to rugged uplands which themselves slope to marshy coastal plains around the southern region of the Gulf of Carpentaria.

Queensland is known as the 'Sunshine State' but weather conditions vary dramatically from the coastal plains to the drier inland and from the temperate south to the tropical north. Along the coast in winter it is mild and mostly dry, with occasional frosty nights. The capital – Brisbane – averages 7.1 hours of sunshine a day in winter, more than any other state capital city. Inland, the winter days are sunny and the nights cold and frosty.

Summer – from December to February – is the wet season, particularly in the tropics. It is then that the monsoons sweep down from Asia. Tropical cyclones can cause flooding rains along the coast and even inland. The Bureau of Meteorology operates a sophisticated cyclone warning system so that preparations can be made for cyclonic weather before it hits.

Queensland has the widest range of scenery of any Australian state yet most of its two million-plus people live in three centres: the capital, Brisbane; the millionaire's holiday resort called Surfers Paradise south of Brisbane, and the Sunshine Coast, a holiday area north of the capital. The two resorts have golden beaches.

The state has many other things including the world's largest sand island, called Frazer Island. It has 300 national parks and is also the land where *Waltzing Matilda* was created.

The state also gave the nation Qantas, the country's world airline, the Flying Doctor Service and fostered the beginnings of the Australian Labor Party.

Qantas, which stands for Queensland and Northern Territory Aerial Service, was born out of a chance meeting in an outback hotel. Two young ex-Royal Flying Corps officers – P.J. McGuinness and Hudson Fysh – were asked by the Commonwealth Government in 1919 to carry out a ground survey for the Darwin-Longreach leg of the $20,000 competition for the first London-Australia flight, and McGuiness accidentally met a Cloncurry grazier, Fergus McMaster, whose car had broken down. When McMaster walked to the hotel for help the first person he met was the former flyer, who helped repair the broken-down vehicle. McMaster shared the two young men's vision of an air service and the following year they formed Qantas. The company began with a staff of three, two war-type biplanes and a capital of £6,307. Today, Qantas has assets running into hundreds of millions of dollars and more than a score of wide-bodied jet aircraft.

In 1912, an organisation named AIM – The Australian Inland Mission – was formed to care for people living in the outback, following a report by the Reverend John Flynn. This led to the establishment of the Flying Doctor Service at inland Cloncurry. The service was later incorporated into The Royal Flying Doctor Service. As part of the aerial medical service, AIM evolved the ingenious midget pedal wireless set, which quickly helped to form the basis of an outback communication network. The Reverend Flynn was the Superintendent of AIM until his death in 1951.

Brisbane was established as a penal settlement in 1824 and it was not until 1842 that free settlers were permitted closer than 80 kilometres to today's capital. Because of this restriction, early free settlers moved west of Brisbane to the Darling Downs, near Warwick, and also to the northwest of the settlement.

Brisbane is a city of hills, with the Brisbane River winding through it. It has many homes on stilts because of its sub-tropical climate.

The renowned explorer Sir Thomas Mitchell said 'you may discover another Australia but you will never discover another Darling Downs'. A century and a half later the Downs, west of Brisbane , are 15,000 square kilometres of bounteous, black soil manicured into a pattern of fields stretching over the horizon. Not only is it Queensland's main wheat region but there are other crops, too, including cotton, sorghum, sunflower and other oil seeds, beans and large numbers of dairy and beef cattle as well as sheep.

Queensland is also sugar cane country. But the backbreaking days, when men toiled for hours under a hot sun, have now gone because of machinery. But those rough days are remembered in the play *The Summer of the Seventeenth Doll*, which was based on Queensland's cane cutters.

Although it was one of the last states created, Queensland has contributed much to the nation's settlement; particularly the explorers, who endured many hardships to trek west and north. Pioneering was more difficult than in the southern states because of the fierce Aborigines encountered. The Aborigines fought hard to retain their land as the white man moved in. There were many clashes. Although the Aborigines killed many white men, they themselves suffered, particularly from punitive parties who killed them at random in revenge for earlier attacks.

Queensland is a beef state and it supplies more than 40 per cent of the nation's output. The state's outback has big cattle stations and it surprises many overseas visitors that all Australians are not like the bronzed, sunburnt people that work there. The only time most Australians see a cattle station is on television, from the comfort of their urban homes.

In Queensland's northwest is the town of Mt Isa, which is one of the world's richest fields of silver, copper, lead and zinc. Situated in Australia's far north, on the western side of Cape York Peninsula, is Weipa. Once a mission area it is, today, the site of an industrial town servicing the region's bauxite mines.

Queensland's output of goods and services is maintaining a growth rate higher than the rest of Australia. Her economy is based on an abundance of natural resources which include extensive energy sources for the processing of raw materials, which boost investment and employment opportunities in the state.

In 1982 Queensland staged the XII Commonwealth Games, which were dubbed the 'Friendly Games'. As she rolled into Queen Elizabeth II Stadium, Matilda – a giant, electrical, winking kangaroo – the Games' mascot – captured the hearts of everyone who was to compete, watch or take part in the Games.

The Northern Territory stretches from the 'Red Heart' of this sunburnt land, known as the Centre, to the Top End about 2,000 kilometres to the north. It is an unbelievable land of contrast and grandeur. It encompasses vast and timeless deserts with endless horizons; lush tropical rainforests alive with nature; massive tablelands, and towering monoliths and mountain ranges thrown up by the giant forces of nature 600 million years ago. It has been the home of Aborigine tribes for thousands of years and it has landmarks containing ancient tribal symbols of myth and Dreamtime.

The adventuring of the pioneers in the last century can be seen in towns like Darwin, Alice Springs, Tennant Creek and Katherine; each of which possess its own, unique character.

Despite its desert background, the Northern Territory has become a tourist playground, offering the traveller every convenience and comfort; from casinos, restaurants, air-conditioned hotels in the cities, to the small, traditional, friendly hospitality of smaller towns. It is the land for the photographer, the hunter, the fisherman, the wildlife enthusiast, the adventurer. One can rough it on safari or see it from the luxury of an air-conditioned coach or aircraft. Flora and fauna abound and thousands of unique species inhabit its jungles, grasslands and national parks.

The visitor will find the people have an unusual life style and many unique festivals, including the 'Henley on Todd' regatta, which is held annually on a dry river bed near Alice Springs. The 'yachts' are fully rigged but have neither deck nor bottom. The crew stand inside, lifting the bottomless craft thigh high, and charge through the soft sand of the Todd River, first perhaps on a straight beat to windward, tacking into the wind, and then back again. It is perilous 'sailing' and hilarious to watch. The capital, Darwin, the northern gateway to Australia, also has a unique annual event; the beer can regatta. Boats competing in the main event are required to derive 90 per cent of their flotation from empty beer cans.

Back at Alice Springs they have the annual camel cup. There is also the Bangtail muster, which originated from the cattle stations and the stock camps when the tips of the tails of the cattle were collected after mustering to count the number of head.

On the May Day holiday there is a procession of floats through Alice Springs with sports and games in the afternoon. There is also the rodeo, the bougainvillea festival – which captures all the beauty of tropical Darwin – and the Alice Art Prize, which is a major art exhibition with entries from Australian as well as overseas artists.

Darwin – destroyed by Cyclone Tracy in 1974 – has been rebuilt into a modern city of more than 55,000 people of all creeds and colours. This was the second time that death and destruction had hit Darwin from the skies. The city was bombed 64 times by Japanese aircraft during the war and destruction was widespread. The worst raid was on February 19, 1942 in which 172 people were killed.

Three attempts failed before Darwin was established in 1869, its future becoming more assured with the building of the trans-continental telegraph line, and the gold finds at Pine Creek created a much-needed impetus. At the same time the foundations of the cattle industry were laid with the overlanding of mobs from Queensland and South Australia. Properties are large, averaging 2,500 square kilometres but the land can support an average of only four beasts to the square kilometre. Mining leads the economy with the massive uranium reserves on the Alligator Rivers.

Before self-government was granted in 1978 the Northern Territory had many guardians. First taken over as part of New South Wales, it was then mothered by South Australia from 1863. In 1911, responsibility for government passed to the Commonwealth, which held the reins for more than 60 years. The Territory's voice in the Federal House of Representatives was not fully heard before 1968 when the member was granted full voting rights.

Despite their small number – there are about 130,000 – Territorians have made their mark in Australia, particularly on life in the outback. Aboriginal Albert Namatjira, and his fellow artists of the Aranda School of Water Color Painting, brought a new dimension to the already strong tradition of Aboriginal art. It was also in the far Outback that Harold Lasseter died searching for a fabled reef of gold.

The Gove Peninsula on the northeastern tip of Arnhem Land is bounded by white, sandy beaches. Inland there is lush, tropical bush through which numerous rivers flow. It is the centre of massive bauxite mining with major facilities to handle the millions of tonnes of bauxite and alumina exported every year. It is also the traditional home of many Aboriginal tribes whose art is renowned throughout the world.

In Darwin there is a memorial to the workmen who built the

overland telegraph line from Adelaide to Darwin, and who completed the epic task in 1872, enabling the first message to be sent between London and Adelaide. Another landmark is the Stuart Memorial, which honours explorer John McDouall Stuart, who left Adelaide on October 22, 1861, and reached a point east of Darwin in July 1862. This epic south-to-north crossing of the continent became the route for the overland telegraph and the Stuart Highway.

The World Heritage Council has recently listed Kakadu National Park, a 6,000 square kilometre area rich in natural and cultural heritage. The park, 220 kilometres east of Darwin, lies between the south Alligator and the east Alligator Rivers. Its landscape is the product of a continuing weathering, erosion and sedimentation over some two million years. Some Aboriginal rock paintings found in this area date back 18,000 years.

Doctor's Gully is a favourite feeding ground for fish. Twenty years ago this activity began when a few mullets appeared. Now, at feeding times, the tranquillity is temporarily shattered by frenzied fish fighting for bread thrown into the water by visitors.

The Northern Territory has a crocodile farm 30 minutes drive south of Darwin. A sign at the gate warns that trespassers could be eaten. It is no idle threat as inside lurk 1,000 crocodiles, ranging in length from a few centimetres to more than four metres. Visitors can wander the estate in safety, never more than a few metres away from 1,000 sets of beady eyes and chomping jaws. The smiling reptiles are all guests of a 1.2 million dollar crocodile hotel which covers nearly 50 hectares and has been funded in part by the Northern Territory Government.

In the Centre is the Ayers Rock monolith, a huge block of sandstone which rises abruptly out of the mulga plain, presenting an awesome spectacle. Its fiery red glow at sunset draws hordes of tourists. Ayres Rock rears 348 metres above the plain. It is almost nine kilometres around the base. The rock dates back almost 600 million years to the Pre-Cambrian era. Subsequent earth movements have tilted the rock until its strata are now vertical. Wind and water over millions of years have created caverns and overhangs. After rain, water tumbles along the channels and down falls which drop elegantly to the plain and irrigates a strip around the base where vegetation flourishes, attracting animals and birds.

On the horizon are the Olgas, a jumble of some 30 brilliant red monoliths scattered across the plain within Uluru Park and known to Aborigines as *Katatjuta* – 'mountain of the heads'. When Ernest Giles came upon them in 1872, he likened them to 'monstrous pink haystacks' and then in more lyrical terms he commented 'time, the old and dim magician has laboured ineffectually here...Mount Olga has remained as it was born'.

Down the track from Darwin is Katherine and close to the town is the Katherine Gorge, which is part of the Katherine Gorge National Park. It is one of the most spectacular natural attractions in Australia's Northern Territory. The river's twisting course flows through a series of deep gorges with gigantic natural rock walls, which form fascinating shapes and feature some of Australia's best Aboriginal rock paintings. The canyon created by the Katherine River is a chain of 13 separate chasms.

Rain, either too much or too little, dominates the Northern Territory. The hot, monsoonal Top End, green and tropical, is washed by the warm waters of the Timor and Arafura Seas and life is governed by the wet and dry seasons. In contrast, to the south are the deserts and outback of the arid Red Centre, a land worn to its bones by millions of years of erosion.

The northwesterlies begin blowing in November, bringing the monsoonal downpours that give the north its annual 1,500mm of rain in only four months. In April the skies clear and the waters retreat.

The Arnhem Land Plateau is an ancient, untouched world of high rocky plain, mountain and gorge. Almost all is reserved for the Aborigines.

The plateau was part of the land bridge across which the Aborigines came to Australia more than 50,000 years ago. Down through time they have left a treasure house of their art, which records in pictures their heritage and beliefs. There are more than 300 galleries described as the most numerous and beautiful in Australia. The area is rich in uranium with 20 per cent of the world's high grade reserves.

Canberra, the national capital, is a planned city. It has been built on a plain surrounded by low, forested hills. Canberra's design resulted from a competition held by the Australian Government in 1911. The winning entry was submitted by an American, Walter Burley Griffin, in conjunction with his wife, Marion Mahony.

Canberra, today, basically follows Burley Griffin's plans. This provided for two main areas – consisting of circular roads linked by radial crossroads – to be separated by an artificial lake. This was formed when the Scrivener Dam was built across the Molonglo River in 1963 and the lake was named after Burley Griffin.

The Australian Capital Territory was ceded to the Commonwealth by New South Wales in 1911 and Canberra was formally inaugurated in 1913. Although Federation occurred in 1901, the Federal Parliament sat in Melbourne until 1927 when the new Parliament House in Canberra was opened by the Duke of York, later King George VI.

The area had first been settled in 1820 and today the capital is known as the 'city of trees'. Each new landowner is offered, at no cost, 50 trees and shrubs and the city and suburbs already have more than eight million trees.

The ACT itself covers 2,330 square kilometres, much of it pleasantly rolling plains, which makes it ideal land for the sheep industry.

Apart from the Government offices and embassies, Canberra has many places of interest. By the 21st century it is expected to have more than 500,000 citizens. The Governor-General lives in the 40-room mansion called Yarralumla.

One of Canberra's spectacular tourist attractions is the Carillon sited near Lake Burley Griffin. The Carillon was a gift from the British Government in 1963 to mark Canberra's 50th anniversary. Its 53 bells (a true carillon consists of at least 23) are tuned over 4.5 octaves and weigh between seven kilogrammes and seven tonnes. The lowest note is produced by the bourdon, the heaviest bell. The instrument, which originated in Flanders in the 15th century and is played with a baton and pedal keyboard, has an official carillonist. The player uses fists and feet to strike levers and pedals attached to clappers. Westminster chimes peal every 15 minutes and on Sunday afternoons, recitals are relayed for broadcast in the city's centre.

Apart from the world-acclaimed War Memorial, Canberra has an art gallery with more than 70,000 works which have been gathered over many years. There are 11 galleries, one of which houses the controversial $1.3 million painting *Blue Poles* by Jackson Pollock. The Australian works include Aboriginal art.

Canberra is also home to the Mt Stromlo Observatory which, in recent years, has been involved in a study of the evolution and structure of the stars; the National Botanic Gardens, which is devoted entirely to native flora; the High Court of Australia, a modern glass and concrete building; and, of course, Parliament House with its colonnaded King's Hall lined with portraits of the Queen, governors-general, prime ministers and other prominent parliamentarians. A short distance from Canberra is the Tidbinbilla Space Centre, which is an important communications link in American space travel.

The great buildings and magnificent layout of Canberra are the physical embodiment of the Commonwealth. The material achievements of Canberra symbolise the achievements of the nation which came into being in 1901.

Despite occasional discontent in the states, Federation is firmly established and has come a long way since talk of it began about the middle of the 19th century. At first there was little interest, mainly because the other colonies believed Federation would enable New South Wales to dominate the nation's economic and political life.

However, events north of Australia helped the cause. Germany annexed northeastern New Guinea in 1884, France established bases in the New Hebrides in 1886 and the fear of foreign powers increased when Japan attacked China in 1894.

In 1889, a British officer, Major General Edwards, issued a warning on Australia's poor defences and urgently recommended the formation of a national army.

The spark became a flame in the 1880s when the three-times Premier of New South Wales, Sir Henry Parkes, made a political speech in the New South Wales country town of Tenterfield, in which his theme was 'Dominion Parliament in the Dominion of Australia'. Sir Henry said that the United States had about the same population as Australia – at that time it was between three and four million – when they formed their great commonwealth. 'Surely what the Americans have done in war Australians can do in peace', he said. The speech had repercussions throughout the land, but many years passed before the Commonwealth of Australia was proclaimed on January 1, 1901. By then Sir Henry was dead.

Before Federation, gold had certainly caused Australia's 19th-century population boom. In 1858 the nation's population reached one million; in another 20 years it had doubled.

By the 1850s, much of Australia's exploration had been done and the next 50 years saw all the states strive to establish an equitable system of land ownership and better communications. Railways began to fan out through the nation, replacing a mode of travel that for years had been by coach over rough bush tracks, with goods being transported by bullock wagons and paddle steamers.

For many years after the states gained self-government there were no organised political parties and there were many ministries and coalitions. It was not until 1889, in New South Wales, that an election was fought with political organisations comparable to those of today. The Australian Labor Party is the country's oldest political party, although its present title was not adopted throughout the nation until 1918.

By 1910 Labor had won a majority of seats in the Federal Parliament and in the parliaments of some of the states. Soon afterwards, the party began to show a tendency towards disunity and internal disruption which has continued to blot its history. Between 1910 and 1972 it held office in Federal Parliament for a total of only 16 years. However, over the same period it was much more successful in some of the states and it has always remained one of the largest, and usually the largest, single party in the country.

In 1929 James Scullin became the first Australian-born Labor Prime Minister. His government did not last long because Australia was suffering from a severe depression. Hundreds of thousands were out of work and many homeless people lived in parks or makeshift homes.

For years there had been efforts to form a central organisation for all trade unions but this did not succeed until 1927, when the Australian Council of Trade Unions was formed. It only represented 10 per cent of unionists before

Commanding spectacular views over King George Sound, Albany *previous page* has the distinction of being Western Australia's oldest town. Bunbury *facing page* is an important southwestern port town, serving the area's timber and farming industries. *Above* Pemberton.

Founded by Captain Stirling in 1829, Perth *these and previous pages* **has blossomed into one of the nation's most beautiful cities. Recent discoveries of mineral wealth have ensured the continued prosperity of the 'City of Light'.** *Overleaf left* **the towering business district.** *Overleaf, right* **the city's modern face seen across the Swan River.**

These pages **the wide expanse of the Swan River seen from Kings Park, near the Narrows, with the Narrows Bridge shown** *facing page.* *Overleaf, left* **Winthrop Hall, part of the University of Western Australia, located in the southern suburb of Crawley.** *Overleaf, right* **St Mary's Cathedral on Victoria Square.**

Above the city seen across Perth Water from South Perth. *Facing page* looking south over the Mitchell Freeway from the grounds of Parliament House. *Overleaf, left* Bridge Street, with Perth Railway Station to the right of picture. *Overleaf, right* a tangled maze of interchanges seen from Kings Park by night.

Among Western Australia's many cherished old buildings dating
back to the colonial days is the lovingly restored Turner's
Cottage *above*, near Serpentine. *Facing page* Queen's Gardens,
where can be seen a replica of London's famous Peter Pan statue.
Overleaf Fremantle Market and a view towards the War Memorial.

Located at the mouth of the Swan River, some 20km southwest of
Perth, Fremantle *these pages* is the largest port in the state.
Facing page the famous Round House Gaol, the state's oldest
building. *Above* a view of the city from the War Memorial.
Overleaf the well-preserved town of York dates back to 1830.

Kalgoorlie *these pages and overleaf* **owes its existence to Paddy Hannan's fortuitous discovery, in 1893, of rich gold deposits. A large number of fine, ornate old buildings bear testimony to the town's prosperous past, and whilst gold continues to be mined, pastoralism has become increasingly important to the region.**

Paddy Hannan may have been the 'father' of Kalgoorlie *these pages*
but it is thanks to the ingenuity of C.Y. O'Connor, who brought
water to the town via a 597km-long pipeline, that the community
was able to survive in the inhospitable semi-desert surroundings.
Overleaf the Pinnacles, in Nambung National Park.

Facing page **St Francis Xavier's Cathedral in Geraldton** *overleaf,*
**an important port and administration centre for the state's mid-
western region. Because of its fine year-round climate and superb
beaches, the city is also a popular holiday resort.** *Above* **the
Spanish-style church at New Norcia.**

Within the Hamersley Range National Park *these pages and overleaf* **is to be found some of the most spectacular and rugged of Western Australia's scenery. Here can be seen plunging gorges and yawning chasms, and all around the layered, folded red rock exhibits the effects of erosion.**

The area around the town of Kununurra *these pages* is famous for its rugged, coloured hills and valleys, as at Kelly's Knob *facing page*. The town itself is the centre of the vast Ord River irrigation project.

Darwin *these pages* **is a modern, cosmopolitan city whose prosperity is based on the region's vast mineral resources.** *Above and facing page, top right* **Darwin's port.** *Top right* **Christchurch Cathedral.** *Centre right* **the Chinese Temple.** *Top left* **the Law Courts, in the modern Civic Centre complex.** *Left and facing page, top left* **the city centre and Smith Street.** *Facing page, bottom left* **the Stuart Highway on the outskirts of the business district.** *Facing page, bottom right* **the East Point Military Museum in the suburb of Fannie Bay.**

Bottom left the towering red walls of Glen Helen Gorge in the Macdonnell Ranges, west of Alice Springs. At the Top End, near Darwin, the scenery is equally interesting and at Fogg Dam left, below and facing page as well as on the Marakai Plains bottom there is an abundance of colourful flora and fauna.

Like so many of Australia's outback towns, Tennant Creek *these pages*, which lies on the Stuart Highway at the very heart of the Northern Territory, owes its existence and continued prosperity to the presence of gold and other scarce minerals in the surrounding hills. The breeding of livestock, however, is also important to the region's economy, with the Barkly Tableland to the east being considered ideal cattle country. Today, Tennant Creek is a modern, forward-looking town; an attitude that is reflected in the prestigious Civic Centre *left*. Unfortunately, none of the original buildings of the 1920s gold rush days remain, but the old mines are still there to be seen. Also of interest is the Government stamp battery, which is being developed as a tourist attraction and shows visitors how gold is separated from the ore.

At the heart of the forbidding Red Centre, within the Macdonnell Ranges, the town of Alice Springs *these pages*, grew around a watering hole discovered during the construction of the Overland Telegraph Line. *Top left* the Anzac Memorial overlooks the town from Anzac Hill. *Above* the John Flynn Memorial Church, built in memory of the founder of the Royal Flying Doctor Service. *Left* the Control Station for the Flying Doctor Service. *Top right* the Church of the Lady of the Sacred Heart. *Facing page* Alice Springs from Anzac Hill.

Before the completion of the railway in 1929 Afghan camel drivers kept Alice Springs supplied with essentials. Today it is the truckers *this page*, with their huge road trains, who ferry goods the vast distances across the dusty outback roads. *Facing page* scenes of traditional Aboriginal life.

The Old Telegraph Station *this page*, 3km outside modern-day Alice Springs *facing page*, is now a Historical Reserve. The Overland Telegraph Line, which linked Darwin and Adelaide, crossed the Macdonnell Ranges through Heavitree Gap to reach the settlement, which was sited near the actual Alice Springs waterhole. Visitors to the Station can see many reconstructed buildings as well as the kangaroos *bottom right* in the Station's animal compound.

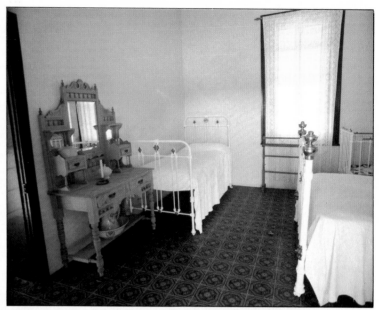

This page the Palm Valley Fauna and Flora Reserve. This oasis, which lies some 140km west of Alice Springs, was discovered by the explorer Ernest Giles in 1872, and is one of the major attractions of the region. Here can be seen crystal clear rock pools shaded by ancient palms reputed to be thousands of years old, amid the twisting gorges of red rock cut by the Finke River. This section of the West Macdonnells is particularly rugged and in places the access tracks are suitable only for four-wheel drive vehicles.

Above Emily Gap, east of Alice Springs; a picnic spot popular with the people of Alice. *Top right* the famous clay sculpture by William Ricketts on the Pitchi-Ritchi Sanctuary. *Top left* the dry, sandy bed of the Todd River, which runs only during periods of heavy rain. *Left* Cutta Cutta Cave, near Katherine.

Right and top right the Finke River Gorge in Ormiston National Park. *Above* Ellery Creek. *Top left* a pool in Glen Helen National Park. Sheer walls that vary in colour according to the light typify majestic Standley Chasm *facing page. Overleaf* Ayers Rock *left* and the Olgas *right*, the Red Centre's most famous sights.

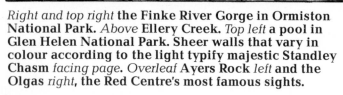

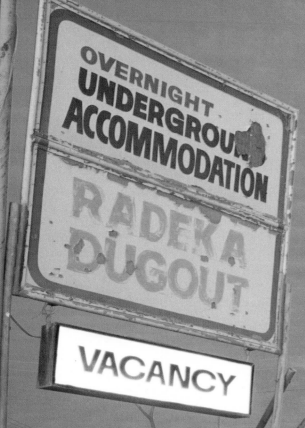

OVERNIGHT
UNDERGROUND
ACCOMMODATION

RADEKA
DUGOUT

VACANCY

ACCOMMODATION
OPALS & JEWELLERY

OPAL

OPAL BUY

THE ALICE EXP
PASSENGER & FREIGHT
9 AM - 5 PM MONDAY TO

BASE STATION

YOUTH
HOSTEL

Visitors
WELCOME

TOURIST
INFORMATION

OPAL
JEWELLERY
TRIPLETS
DOUBLETS
SOLIDS
CUTTING
SOUVENIRS

WORKSHOP

FORD

SLEEP
UNDERGROUND
RADEKA DUGOUT

Previous pages the distinctive, domed Olgas *right* and monolithic Ayers Rock *left* attract thousands of sightseers to the burning wastes of the Centre. Coober Pedy *these pages*, set within the hostile environment of South Australia's outback, is a small opal mining town where most of the inhabitants live in dugouts, to escape the severe heat of the sun.

Whyalla *these pages* is an important industrial centre and port on Spencer Gulf, with the mines at nearby Iron Knob and Iron Baron supplying the city's huge BHP iron and steel works via the special rail links.

Largest town on the Cape Yorke Peninsula, Kadina *these pages* **was once a prominent copper-mining town. Today, it is primarily a shopping and commercial centre with a fine architectural heritage.** *Overleaf* **neighbouring Moonta Bay** *left* **and Port Hughes** *right*.

Straddling the waters of the Torrens River, Adelaide, South Australia's elegant capital is a balanced blend of old and new. *Above* **the city from Montefiore Hill.** *Facing page* **St Peter's Cathedral.** *Overleaf, left* **Hindley Street;** *overleaf, right* **the Festival Centre.**

Facing page **the futuristic shape of the Festival Centre, framed by the graceful Victorian ironwork of the Elder Park bandstand.** *Above and overleaf* **Rundle Mall, Adelaide's major shopping thoroughfare.**

Trams *above* **still rumble through many of Adelaide's wide streets, providing the city with an efficient means of transport.** *Facing page* **Jetty Road in the coastal suburb of Glenelg.** *Overleaf, left* **St Peter's Cathedral.** *Overleaf, right* **the snaking Torrens provides relaxation and recreation for the people of the city.**

Hindmarsh Square *above and overleaf* **is typical of the many pleasant squares to be found within this park-ringed city.** *Facing page* **the Festival Centre seen across the waters of Lake Torrens.**

Lorne *above*, on the coast of Victoria's Otway region, is among the most attractive of the state's resorts, with fine beaches and splendid hinterland scenery attracting many visitors to the area. *Facing page* the Great Ocean Road near Cape Patton, south of Lorne.

Port Campbell National Park boasts some of the most spectacular coastline in Victoria, with structures such as the Twelve Apostles *above*, **The Arch** *overleaf, left* **and Island Archway** *overleaf, right* **carved from the soft limestone rock by the pounding sea.**

Above **Flagstaff Hill lighthouse, Warrnambool.** A well-known attraction of this popular coastal resort is the Maritime Village, with its restored sailing ships and period buildings. **Port Fairy** *facing page*, a neighbouring resort, is home to a large fishing fleet. *Overleaf, left* **Horsham,** an important town within the Wimmera region. *Overleaf, right* **Portland,** Victoria's oldest permanent settlement.

The mighty Murray *these pages* was once the country's most important transportation route, with fleets of paddle steamers supplying the many towns that lie along its course. Today these vessels, such as the *Coonawara*, which operates out of Mildura *overleaf, right*, are an ideal means of sightseeing. *Overleaf, left* winery near Red Cliffs.

Mildura, *above* **Deakin Street, on the banks of the Murray, as well as being a holiday town, is part of an important wine growing area that has flourished since the development of the irrigation scheme.** *Facing page* **Swan Hill Pioneer Settlement, a recreated 19th-century riverside town. Echuca** *overleaf, left,* **another Murray town, also preserves its river history at the colourful Port of Echuca.** *Overleaf, right* **the Mall, Bendigo.**

Sovereign Hill *this page* near Ballarat is one of the city's most important tourist attractions. This living museum is a major recreation of a goldmining town of last century, where visitors can take a ride on a stagecoach, try their hand at gold panning or visit the fascinating mining museum. A ride on Puffing Billy *facing page* offers unique views of the scenic Dandenongs.

These pages and overleaf **a stone's throw from the bustle of Melbourne's centre, on the shores of Port Phillip Bay, lie a number of superb, sandy beaches that attract sunseekers in their droves and provide for the city-dweller an ideal form of relaxation.**

Bourke Street Mall *above*, **traffic free except for the occasional tram,**
is the pleasant heart of the Melbourne shopping district. *Facing page*
a view down St Kilda Road from the Shrine of Remembrance, with the
futuristic Victorian Arts Centre on the left and St Paul's Cathedral
to the right. *Overleaf* **the graceful Yarra River.**

Above a view of the imposing bulk of Flinders Street
Station, at the intersection of Swanston and Flinders
Streets. *Facing page* Bourke Street Mall, where some of
Melbourne's most fashionable stores are located, and
the elegant facade of Royal Arcade.

The blazing signs and appetizing smells of Melbourne's Chinatown district *above* **on Little Bourke Street, are irresistible to lovers of Oriental cuisine.** *Facing page* **looking south along Elizabeth Street towards Flinders Street Station.**

Above **enthusiastic scullers on the Yarra River near Alexandra Gardens as seen from Princes Bridge.** *Facing page* **the everyday bustle near Flinders Street Station.**

Kates Cottage *these pages* at Glenrowan, near Wangaratta, is a faithful reconstruction of the Kelly house, built to the same design and dimensions as the original. *Overleaf* narrow Ninety Mile Beach, which separates the Gippsland Lakes from the Tasman Sea.

Above the delicate trace of a lightning bolt rends the sky over a village store near Sale, Gippsland's major city. *Facing page* a suspension bridge spans a densely wooded valley in Bulga National Park, near **Yarram.** *Overleaf, left* **Squeaky Bay** and *overleaf, right* **Norman Bay,** in Wilsons Promontory National Park.

Above **picturesque Hobart, Tasmania's capital city, seen from the suburb of Lindisfarne.**
Facing page **Wrest Point Marina and the Casino.** *Overleaf* **the graceful Tasman Bridge, which spans the Derwent to link the city with its suburbs and airport to the east.**

Previous page, left **Bellerive, a Hobart suburb, seen from Rosny Hill.** *Previous page, right* **a panoramic view of Hobart. Thredbo, in the Snowy Mountains of New South Wales is a year round holiday resort.** *Above* **the Thredbo Hotel and swimming pool,** *facing page* **the Alpine village seen from the Crackenback chairlift.**

Designed as the 'showpiece of the nation' by Walter Burley Griffin, Canberra is a well laid out, modern city. *Above* **Parliament House;** *facing page* the **Captain Cook Memorial.** *Overleaf* **the city, Lake Burley Griffin and the telecommunications tower on Black Mountain, seen from the air.**

Sport is a particular Australian passion, and Canberra offers top class facilities for all popular forms of physical recreation, from the sedate *facing page* **to the more energetic** *above*.

The magnificent Australian War Memorial *above*, which honours the nation's war dead, is amongst Canberra's top tourist attractions. The building houses a fine collection of military relics. *Facing page* looking towards Parliament House from the War Memorial.

Facing page **Banna Avenue in Griffith, a town which serves a major fruit growing and processing region. Much of the local grape crop** *overleaf, right* **goes to the many wineries in the region.** *Overleaf, left* **fruit drying near Wentworth.** *Above* **Wagga Wagga, an important town on the Murrumbidgee River.**

Once a thriving mining community, Silverton became a ghost town almost overnight when the majority of the population deserted the town in favour of the rich silver deposits of Broken Hill. Today, the town attracts visitors with its historic gaol *these pages.*

To the many visitors who come to see a dusty, ramshackle mining town, Broken Hill, with its many fine buildings and bustling atmosphere, is a pleasant surprise. *Facing page* the Post Office tower on Argent Street and *above* Sulphide Street Station, now a museum and information centre.

Bathurst *facing page and previous pages, left* **and Orange** *previous pages, right* **are** two long-established cities that serve the important pastoral and fruit growing Central Western Region. *Above* the Mt Panorama motor racing circuit near Bathurst.

Above the Sydney Harbour Bridge and ferry-boat seen from Pier One. *Facing page* the spectacular Opera House, which stands on Bennelong Point, has become one of the city's major landmarks. *Overleaf, left* aerial view of Sydney's western suburbs and *overleaf, right* the city, with Walsh Bay and Darling Harbour in the foreground.

Above the Centrepoint Tower seen from Hyde Park. *Facing page* the Harbour Bridge and Opera House; symbols of a dynamic city. *Overleaf, left* elegant Strand Arcade. *Overleaf, right* older properties typical of Sydney's inner suburbs.

Facing page **Sydney's modern, high-rise business district reflects the prosperity of the Premier State.** *Above* **a view of the city from the Victoria Road at Wrights Point.** *Overleaf, left* **Chinatown.** *Overleaf, right* **the Pier One shopping and entertainment complex.**

World-famous Bondi Beach *above,* **and Bronte Beach** *facing page* **are just two of the many fine beaches where Sydneysiders can indulge their passion for sun, sand and sea.** *Overleaf, left* **the recreated lumbering settlement of Timbertown, near Wauchope.** *Overleaf, right* **the important industrial city of Newcastle.**

Both Coffs Harbour *facing page* **and the larger town of Port Macquarie** *above* **to the south, cater for the seasonal influx of holidaymakers attracted by the many fine, sandy beaches. For those seeking a more commercialised seaside vacation, no other resort can rival the attractions of Queensland's Gold Coast** *overleaf.*

City of the Gold Coast, the strip of land stretching between Southport and Coolangatta, is devoted to catering for the holidaymaker and embraces the well-known resort of Surfers Paradise *these pages and overleaf.*

Beaches are not the only attractions for the visitor to Queensland's southern coast. At Southport, Sea World offers a variety of amusements, including a replica of the *Endeavour facing page* while colourful birds, such as the Rainbow lorikeet *above*, can be seen at the Currumbin Bird Sanctuary.

Victoria Bridge *facing page* **and the Captain Cook Bridge** *above* **are two of the newest spans across the Brisbane River, linking central Brisbane with its southern suburbs.** *Overleaf, left* **a view of the city across Town Reach from Kangaroo Point at dusk.** *Overleaf, right* **once the tallest of the city's structures City Hall, a Brisbane landmark, is now dwarfed by many modern office blocks.**

Above **a view of the modern business district, seen from Story Bridge at Petrie Bight. The old Customs House building can be seen on the right of the picture.** *Facing page and overleaf, right* **City Hall, which fronts onto the open space of King George Square.** *Overleaf, left* **Queen Street Mall; a popular, traffic free shopping precinct.**

The carefully tended grounds of the old Botanic Gardens, at the southern tip of the City district, are overshadowed by contrasting shapes of Parliament Houses both old and new *above. Facing page* pleasure craft ride at anchor on the Town Reach stretch of the river. *Overleaf* abseilers pause for a meal *left* before descending the spectacular Ballanjui Falls *right*, in Lamington National Park.

Facing page the Sunshine Pineapple Plantation, near the town of Nambour, is one of the major tourist attractions on the Sunshine Coast. Panoramic views of the plantation are to be had from the top of the Big Pineapple. *Above* fine Victorian buildings, with their delicate ironwork tracery, are typical of Rockhampton, the 'beef capital' of Australia. *Overleaf* the tough outdoor life can be experienced first hand, at the Silver Hills Inland Resort.

Giant smoke stacks stand silhouetted against the darkening sky at Mount Isa *previous page,*
left. **Townsville** *previous page, right,* **which is linked to Mount Isa by rail, is one of the**
state's major ports, and handles much of the ore from the mines of the northwest. *These pages*
the lush green vegetation and warm, turquoise waters of the Cairns region. *Overleaf* **Millaa**
Millaa Falls *left* **and Kuranda Railway Viaduct** *right* **in the scenic Atherton Tableland.**

The golden beaches of the Cairns *above* **and Port Douglas** *facing page* **regions, backed by dense, tropical forests, are amongst the finest in the world.** *Overleaf, left* **a meandering river cuts through a dense rainforest in the vicinity of Cairns** *overleaf, right* **'capital' of the tropical north of Queensland.**

Founded in 1876 to service the mining areas of the north, Cairns *these pages and overleaf* soon turned its attention to agriculture, becoming one of the country's major sugar growing regions. Sugar remains important to the city, but to the visitor Cairns is primarily a stepping off point for the wonders of the Atherton Tableland and the Great Barrier Reef.

Heron Island *these pages*, off the coast of Gladstone, is one of hundreds of islands that dot the warm waters of the Barrier Reef. This tiny, densely-wooded coral cay is a sanctuary for a surprising variety of marine birds.